CHINA DIARY: AFTER MAO

China Diary:
After Mao
Charlotte Y. Salisbury

WALKER AND COMPANY
NEW YORK

For Harrison

First published in the United States of America in 1979 by the Walker Publishing Company, Inc.

Published simultaneously in Canada by Beaverbooks, Limited, Pickering, Ontario.

ISBN: 0-8027-0621-5

Library of Congress Catalog Card Number: 78-70932

Printed in the United States of America

10   9   8   7   6   5   4   3   2   1

PREFACE

In 1972 I accompanied my husband, Harrison Salisbury, associate editor of the *New York Times,* on a trip to the Peoples' Republic of China. His book *To Peking and Beyond* and my *China Diary* described that trip.

In 1977 we went again on a reporting trip even though Harrison had retired from the paper. On both visits we were fortunate to be able to travel alone with highly intelligent guides who were enormously helpful and of whom we became very fond.

This is the story of our latest visit to that fascinating country.

With President Carter's dramatic action in recognizing the Peoples' Republic of China as the only legal China, a whole new era has been ushered in. For the first time in thirty years the Chinese and the Americans will have a chance to behave normally towards each other. No longer will contact be limited to guides and interpreters on business or tour groups. We will have chances to get to know Chinese people and they will have opportunities to get to know us.

There will be all kinds of changes and differences. Chinese students will be coming to the United States to study in our universities. Technical missions will be sent here to study our industry, to work in our factories. Scientists will work in our institutes. The Chinese will learn "the best from the West" as Mao suggested but did not permit. American specialists will be going to China to study their methods, to learn what we can from them and to share our knowledge with them. There will be an enormous expansion of trade between our countries, an increase in tourists as fast as new hotels and facilities can be built. Already American firms have contracted to build and equip hotels, even one in Llasa in Tibet.

Cultural exchanges will be increased. Last year *Love Story* was translated into Chinese because it was on a best-seller's list. Perhaps with increasing understanding of our culture more representative American literature will find its way to China. Literature, music, painting—all our arts will probably eventually be heard and seen in Peking, and we can expect more of theirs from them.

Chinese women will come over on a serious mission, will visit our stores, see our fashions and what we are wearing and how we do our hair. Recently, we hear, some Chinese women have begun to wear skirts and curl their hair. People are even talking about the Americanization of China.

I can't believe that will ever happen and I hope the

Chinese will stay Chinese and our two peoples will get along, each of us keeping our special identity. In that way we will have much more to give to each other.

There have been many changes in China since 1949, and I am not inclined to think that our returning to normal relations means there will be no more changes internally. Fox Butterfield, in *The New York Times*, quotes a Chinese woman as saying in respect to the recent multitude of posters put up in Peking demanding human rights and democracy, "No one believes it can go on very long. Things have changed so many times before. It is like watching another play."

But with diplomatic and business relations restored, we can look forward to, and hope for, increasing understanding and friendship with some of the most gifted and attractive people in the world.

New York City
December 16, 1978

NAMES THAT ARE MENTIONED OFTEN

Mao Tse-tung	Chairman of the People's Republic of China, died September 1976
Chou En-lai	Premier of the People's Republic of China, died January 1976
Madame Soong, or Soong Ching-ling	Widow of Sun Yat-sen, founder of the Chinese Revolution. She is vice-chairman of the People's Republic of China
Hua Kuo-feng	Present chairman of the People's Republic of China
Teng Hsiao-ping	Vice-chairman of the People's Republic of China
Yeh Chien-ying	Vice-chairman of the People's Republic of China
Li Hsien-nien	Vice-chairman of the People's Republic of China
Wang Tung-hsing	Vice-chairman of the People's Republic of China

Liu Shao-chi	President of China, leader of the group displaced by the Cultural Revolution
Lin Piao	Minister of Defense, designated heir of Mao. Died in a mysterious airplane crash in 1971. Subsequently charged with plotting against Mao
Mr. Ma	Member of the Press Department
Mr. Mao	Our interpreter and companion in 1977
Yao Wei	Our interpreter and companion in 1972
Members of The Gang of Four:	
Chiang Ching	Wife of Chairman Mao and leader of the Gang of Four
Chang Chun-chiao	Party Secretary of Shanghai
Yao Wen-yuan	Writer for the Shanghai newspaper *Wen Wei Pao*
Wang Hung-wen	Head of the Textile Workers' Union

Sunday, August 21, 1977

"RED FLAGS are blowing in the hot wind, loud music hits my ears, swarms of young Chinese men and women stand at posts or move slowly about helping travelers here and there, and I am walking across the covered railroad bridge, doorway to the People's Republic of China."

That is what I wrote five years ago when I had taken the train from Hong Kong, on my way to meet my husband in Peking.

How different our approach is this time. In 1972 visitors to China came through Hong Kong to Shum Chun, on the border, and on to Canton by train. From there they went by Chinese train or plane to their destination. Nowadays five different airlines fly to Peking from Tokyo alone, and Shanghai also has an international airport. Tonight we are on an Iranian airplane flying from Tokyo. Except for the security men we might be on any international flight anywhere in the world. There is caviar, champagne, and sophisticated stewardesses. But several sinister-looking men are constantly walking from one end of the plane to the other, stopping often to give each passenger a fierce look from their handsome, scary faces. This plane comes from Teheran; we were delayed four hours in Tokyo, and even our big bags that go in the luggage compartment were searched before being put on. We are wondering if some poor man is waiting for us in Peking and whether he can find out that we are already nearly five hours late.

Lots of other things are different, too, since June and July 1972. Nixon had made his triumphant trip to China that March; the atmosphere was exciting and full of hope that our countries' differences would soon be resolved; Harrison was only the fourth person from the *New York Times* to go to China, I the third *Times* wife. Mao, though old and feeble, was alive and seeing the most important visitors; Chou En-lai was very much alive and entertaining foreigners at sumptuous banquets almost nightly; the horrors and anarchy of the Cultural Revolution were, if not over, at least under some sort of surface control; Chiang Ching was in the background.

Now Mao and Chou are dead; Chiang Ching is under arrest along with her three closest cohorts (the Gang of Four). Chiao Kuang-hua, who was foreign minister and whom we liked enormously, is out, disgraced. He made the mistake of marrying a friend of Chiang Ching, so he fell out of favor with the group that is now in power. Huang Hua, who was ambassador to the United Nations, is now foreign minister. Hua Kuo-feng is chairman (appointed vice-chairman by Mao before his death, to prevent his wife from taking control?). Mr. Teng Hsiao-ping, who has already been out of favor three times before, is currently in as first vice-chairman. There must be other changes we don't know about.

Things are different at home, too. Nixon is out, disgraced, and all his White House circle. Ford was president, went to China, and accomplished nothing. Now we have Carter. Taiwan is still a stumbling block. There seems no way to resolve that situation to everyone's satisfaction. The good feelings have cooled.

But the biggest change of all is that the Vietnam War is over, finally ground to a halt in 1973. It was a paramount issue on our last visit. Everyone talked about it; everyone felt relations between China and the United States would be much easier once it was over. I remember Chou En-lai devoting the whole time we were drinking tea before dinner one evening to the war and the tragedy of it. He became so emotional he could hardly continue, and I swear he had tears in his eyes when he spoke about the suffering of the Vietnamese people.

And my own feelings are different. I don't feel any excitement. I can't imagine what we will be able to see and do that will be new. The Chinese wrap us in a cocoon of their making. We have a guide who is always with us; we may go to new places, but I bet we won't go to Tibet or to Sinkiang, near the Russian border, where Harrison wants to go. We will hear the same old reasons—"there are not proper facilities; it is too high, too hot, too cold." It will be the same old routine, the same factories, communes, nurseries, kindergartens, schools, universities. The same conversations about how terrible life was before Liberation, how wonderful it is now, how the thoughts of

Chairman Mao have made everyone work better, live better, and even made vegetables grow better. Well, we shall see. We will be in Peking in a couple of hours.

Monday, August 22,
at the Min Zu Hotel

AT THE AIRPORT the first thing I noticed is that the Chinese are obviously much more used to visitors than they were five years ago. We passed through Customs, Health, and Passport inspection just as if we were in any country where foreign travelers arriving is an everyday occurrence. Last time, as I remember, it was informal and unworldly.

At the last gate a tall, very thin man was waiting for us, Mr. Mao Kuo-hua (as if an American had both the first and last names of our former and present presidents with an ordinary name in the middle, that is, Ford Smith Carter, Hua being the name of the current chairman of the Peoples' Republic of China). He had come to greet us five hours before and had been waiting ever since. The patience of the Chinese is something I envy. He was cheerful and smiling and said that our friend Yao Wei, who had been our constant companion on our first visit, was in Canton and very sorry he couldn't meet us.

We collected our bags and drove in along the tree-lined road to the city. The trees have grown enormous. It was fun to recognize corners and buildings on the way. We saw many people playing cards under streetlights even at that late hour, something we don't remember seeing before—gambling perhaps?

When we arrived at the hotel at 1:30 A.M. we saw Fox Butterfield, the *New York Times* man in Hong Kong, who is here to cover Secretary of State Vance's visit. Vance arrives tomorrow for talks and goodwill. Fox was standing alone in the courtyard looking harassed and wan. He told us that Mr. Liu, of the Press Department of the Foreign Office, had been bawling him out for three hours about the attitude of the *New York Times* and his articles. I gather it started because there was something wrong with Fox's press card for sending cables, but that was probably just a good excuse. He was a sad sight. I noticed that the driver of our car coming in from the airport wore white gloves. Also, he did not help with the luggage either there or here when we arrived. We have two big bags, a small, overnight-size bag, H.'s briefcase, and a typewriter. So far nothing is too heavy, but we do need help. Mr. Mao, Harrison and I carried everything. I hope someone will turn out to be more helpful toward the end of this trip, when we will be laden down with pamphlets and papers and books that will have been given to us by the Chinese.

We got to bed around two and were awakened just after five by the most terrible crashing of cymbals and firecrackers, drums and marching—the third day of the celebration of the Eleventh Party Congress. For miles in every direction soldiers, girls in costumes, acrobats, regular people (workers) marching in their brigades, streamed into the square—about two million people. The Chinese go to bed early and get up early, especially in the summer because it is so hot. But this seems pretty early to be all ready to march in a parade.

I don't think it is possible to convey the noise. We are on the seventh floor, high enough up to have all the sounds merge together and come at us as if from a gigantic trumpet. I remember the everyday noise of cities here, the automobile horns, bicycle bells, whistles, policemen shouting through megaphones, propaganda screaming at us from the ubiquitous loudspeakers. But this parade was louder than the worst noise we heard before, loud and merciless.

The Eleventh Party Congress has just ended. It was the first meeting of the party since Mao died in September 1976. Chairman Hua has obviously taken charge. The Gang of Four is in prison, and the new, more sensible line has been laid down. That is the reason for all this rejoicing.

This hotel, the Min Zu, or Nationalities Hotel, is on the big main street at the opposite end from the Peking Hotel, to the west of Tien An-Men Square. It is simple and bare and stark compared with a similar hotel in New York, say the Biltmore. The walls in the closet are just plain wood, have never been sanded or painted; I killed five cockroaches last night and one this morning and have seen many dead on the floor. During the few hours I was in bed, I heard someone spraying in the hall several times. We never saw any bugs five years ago, either in the

Chien Men Hotel, where we stayed, which is about ten minutes away to the south, or anywhere else. In fact, Harrison kept track of the flies, and in six weeks we saw only forty-three. They used DDT constantly then, and I guess they are not using it so much now, or the bugs have become immune.

Because all the Chinese emphasis is on Secretary Vance's visit, we are not starting our own trip until he leaves, in five days. The American correspondents who are here to cover his activities are staying at this hotel, and we are going to be included in most of the activities if we so wish. Harrison is anxious to get on with our own business, but I think it is wonderful. I have never been in on a state visit of anyone anywhere, and I am impressed by how many journalists are here and how many cars and guides and interpreters it involves. Some correspondents came with Vance today, and some, like Fox, came up from Hong Kong, where they are stationed.

Each journalist has to have a press card with picture, name, and the publication he or she works for. The Chinese have given me one—my first—in a bright red plastic case saying that I am an "independent journalist." So I can go everywhere H. does now, at least in China.

After our rude awakening this morning we had some coffee in our room and went down to breakfast around eight. We sat in a dining room especially reserved for American guests. The Japanese visitors were in another dining room by themselves. Fox and several other correspondents joined us, and we talked about whether anything will really come of Vance's visit. Most think not much. Breakfast consisted of a dish of lichi fruit, three fried eggs each, that great toast I remember so well, toasted over a real flame, butter, jam, and a piece of pastry. The coffee was good, a change from five years ago. We always bring instant coffee with us no matter where we go, and in our room in this hotel we have hot water in a thermos (as in all Chinese hotels), tea, little candies, cigarettes, and fresh fruit.

After breakfast, with our interpreter Mr. Mao, whose name we are not likely to forget, we got into a small green car with a sign Number Sixty-one on it and drove in a procession out to the airport to meet Vance. I can't believe there were sixty-one cars, yet there were quite a few ahead and several behind us and we went in strict numerical order.

At the airport, as so often seems to be the case in China, we sat for one and a half hours drinking soda with the correspondents and journalists who are stationed here, who were also waiting to greet the secretary of state. Finally the big white plane with the American flag painted on the rear and *The United States of America* in huge gold letters from stem to stern, or cockpit to tail, taxied up to the terminal building, impressive and beautiful. So many times in this part of the world I have been ashamed of my country and embarrassed because of the Vietnam War; it was lovely to feel proud and pleased.

Huang Hua and his wife, Madame Ho, were there to greet Mr. and Mrs. Vance, and we shook hands with everyone too. Mrs. Vance said she had my earlier book, *China Diary*, in her bag.

Back at the hotel we had a delicious lunch. Though we sit in a special dining room, we do have Chinese meals. We could have a Chinese breakfast if we wanted to, but we prefer our kind.

The parade was still going on full blast, but somehow, even with all the noise, we managed to get a little sleep before again getting into car sixty-one and being whirled to the Great Hall of the People (only about five minutes away), again in numerical order, to watch Mr. Vance and Huang Hua, with all their aides, sit down at a big conference table and begin their meeting. That was all we were allowed to witness, but we were told that Vance talked for two and a half hours outlining United States foreign policy, and I understand he will have more to say tomorrow. That seems a strange thing to do; certainly the Chinese are well aware of our policy. I thought only dictators talked at length like that, never Americans.

Mr. Mao, Harrison, and I then went to the Temple of Heaven, which is as beautiful as I remember. At this temple sacrifices were made to stimulate a good harvest, and emperors communicated with the gods and paid them homage. The wide walk is being repaved, so it is all torn up and dusty and hard to walk on, and as you look through the gate to the second gorgeous temple, a huge poster of fist-waving workers has been erected, which seems out of place. To the southwest there is a huge mound of earth that was not there five years ago. It conceals an underground-shelter command post and, they say, will be landscaped soon.

Back to the hotel to change for the dinner given by

Huang Hua for Mr. and Mrs. Vance. Again in car sixty-one with Mr. Mao we were taken to the Great Hall. Everyone was invited, all the correspondents, the airplane crew, and naturally everyone at our Liaison Office. The American women had on long dresses, and the Chinese women wore shirts and their usual gray cotton pants with a white or light-colored shirt. Most of the Chinese men wore Mao jackets.

The main table was enormous, with a centerpiece of green feathery leaves and flowers. All the surrounding tables were set for twelve places, so that we could reach all the food in the center and didn't have to be served individually. It was delicious, and there was much too much. I wonder what they do with what's left over.

Both Huang Hua and Vance made bland speeches and toasts—they actually said nothing, but both walked around every table touching glasses with each guest, and the atmosphere was friendly if a bit cool. I sat next to the *Wall Street Journal* man, Keatley. He said that the whole affair was low-key and that rather low-echelon Chinese people, including some academics, were at the main table. If anything is accomplished in the next few days, maybe one of the bigger shots will appear.

In this first day here the main difference in the people I have noticed from five years ago is that women and girls wear more color than formerly; I have seen lots of colored and printed blouses. And people seem plump or rounder. There is a lot of new building in Peking; big apartment houses are being put up all around the city, and on many streets thousands of earth and brick huts have been built since the earthquake last year. Usually they are two-deep, in long rows under the trees between the street and the permanent buildings, leaving some sidewalk for pedestrians. They are called temporary shelters, but many are lived in. We were told that the young people, especially the newly married, prefer living in a hut to sharing a two-room apartment with other members of the family. Some huts have curtains, many have flowers planted around, and I have seen men and women improving the structures by putting up brick walls, windows of glass instead of heavy paper, and roofs made of studier stuff than the flimsy temporary straw.

Tuesday, August 23, 10:30 P.M.

WE SLEPT all right last night, but the noises woke me up all the time. However, I certainly felt better and more rested than yesterday.

At 8:15 we piled into our car with Mr. Mao and drove in proper order nearly two hours out to the Great Wall. Mrs. Vance was going, so we chose to, too. Halfway there something went wrong with the car, and the driver pulled over to the side of the road. Immediately a black car with two Chinese men appeared; we got out of our car and into the black one; our driver did the same. The other men took charge of number sixty-one and obviously got it fixed and back to Peking, because we used it tonight. Mr. Mao said there is always an extra car with drivers on excursions for just such emergencies as this.

As in Peking, there is a lot of new building on the way to the Wall. Also, there seems to be more agriculture—more fruit trees and vegetable fields, especially corn and sorghum. And we passed a huge sand and gravel factory that neither of us remembers. The reservoir near the Ming Tombs (where Chairman Mao worked on the dam along with ordinary workers) seemed fairly full, though our Mr. Mao said it was low, and we could see the high-water marks on the land.

Going to the Great Wall is like going to the Grand Canyon or any notable landmark anywhere. As we approached, many buses and trucks were stopped, too big for anyone to pass them, and the road was jammed completely. For some reason Mrs. Vance and Madame Ho were behind us, and they had to get out and walk the last one-half mile along with everyone else. The road was freshly tarred and gooey in the heat. The parking space was full; tourists, many Japanese but mostly Chinese, were scrambling up, down, in, and all over the wall.

The amazement and wonder at the Great Wall is not dimmed by the second look. It remains one of the greatest sights I have ever seen and seems even more remarkable when I consider that it has been extant since six hundred years before Christ. When we go to Inner Mongolia later on, we will fly over it. I was shocked to see grafitti —characters, letters, and dates—scratched in the stone inside some of the towers. I can't imagine a Chinese doing that—maybe they are Japanese.

We visited the Ming tomb in the valley nearby. We saw this last time, and it is the only tomb that has been opened. (Since this was written, a second tomb has been opened.) There are twelve more in the area, and I suppose one day the Chinese will explore and open them all. Mr. Mao says it is very expensive. Without elaborate precautions artifacts that have been buried for so long disintegrate when exposed to air. It is all too costly for now.

14

Some of the exhibits in the tomb are reproductions—
the originals are in the Forbidden City. But they are
beautiful. Figures in cases show peasant life in simple
shelters and raggedy clothes. The comparison between
the food of the emperor and that of the peasants is
startling: The emperor ate well, off silver and gold plates;
the peasants ate bark, grass, and just a bit of grain, using
leaves or wooden utensils. Figures show peasant
rebellions and the landlords mistreating the people.

There seemed to be more people in the surrounding
park than five years ago, Chinese as well as other foreign
tourists. And it seemed dirtier and dustier.

It was boiling hot, and orange pop and tea in a cool
room in a building near the parking space made a
welcome respite. We came back here for a late lunch,
again very good food. We became very fond of the Chien
Men Hotel in 1972, but so far the food in this hotel is
better.

At 5:00 P.M. Harrison and I went to a reception at the
American Liaison Office given by Leonard Woodcock,
our liaison officer. He is called Ambassador by everyone
except the Chinese, who call him the equivalent of
Liaison Officer, absolutely correct. He has not been an
ambassador to any other place; he resigned from being
head of the United Automobile Workers' Union to come
here. He seems a strange choice—I wonder why Carter
didn't send Mansfield here instead of to Japan. Mansfield
is a Chinese scholar, has taught Chinese history, and has
always been interested in China. We were told that Mr.
Woodcock has a terrible temper and gets violent at times.
But we have also heard that the Chinese like him very

much and feel he understands their point of view about "normalization."

The reception made me ashamed of the way we do, or don't do, things in other countries. Here, in the land of delectable food attractively served even in the most modest places, the hors d'oeuvres were slices of dill pickles on pieces of ham secured by a toothpick, tuna fish on crackers with a slice of olive on top; cold popcorn, tasteless nuts, and little fried fish balls which tasted like fried sawdust and were served with no sauce or dip. Appalling.

Had a cold and not very good Chinese dinner at the International House in the compound set aside for foreigners. All the embassies are in the enclosure, and journalists, radio people, any diplomatic foreigner working in Peking has to live inside this area. There is no mingling with the Chinese. Each gate, even to apartment houses, is guarded by a Chinese soldier, and every visitor is noted. This is not true, however, of people who are referred to as "foreign friends"—who have lived here for many years and have always been sympathetic to the revolution. They, too, have no actual choice but often can persuade the Chinese to give them quarters they prefer. Most live in traditional Chinese houses surrounded by Chinese neighbors. But the beautiful old embassy compounds are being used by the Chinese for their own purposes.

From dinner we went, in proper order again, to the Great Hall to see an acrobatic show given for the Vances. As every Chinese show of any kind that I have ever seen has been, this too was perfection. Many Americans have seen Chinese acrobats by now, either on a visit here or in the United States or on TV. We have wonderful acrobats and precision performers too, but there is something special about the Chinese acts. What they do is so very Chinese—tossing large vases back and forth on their heads or shoulders, dressing up as dancing lions, spinning dishes of water on long strings around and around. Many Chinese were in the audience, mostly students, Mr. Mao said. Girls sat on one side, boys on the other. The act that made them laugh the most was the two men who make wonderful noises of birds, animals, trains. Really amazing. All the acts seemed more professional and sophisticated than what we saw five years ago. Many of the performers bowed to the audience, something unheard of in 1972. Too individual.

Wednesday, August 24, at night

THIS MORNING we went to the Red Star, or China Korean
Friendship Commune. Mrs. Vance was going, so we
followed along in procession, as usual. Only three journalists came (many have been in China before, and these
visits can be repetitious), and Mr. Cannon from the State
Department. We made the usual rounds; first tea with
the head man telling us details about the commune, grain
production, etc. Then a walk to a dam on an irrigation
canal, to a rice field; a walk through a machine shop factory, a visit to a peasant's house and to a clinic.

This commune is a showplace compared with the one
we visited outside Peking five years ago, the Double
Bridge Commune. In the waiting room, or tea-drinking-
reception room, the chairs were large and comfortable
and covered with red—either leather or something that
looked like it. A table stood in front of each chair. The
main-entrance courtyard was paved, flowers grew in all
the little courtyards outside the individual houses, and
the whole place looked spruced up and stylish, not just
workaday and practical.

Eighty-five thousand people live in this commune, in eighteen thousand households. It is divided as most communes and factories are, into three levels, each composed of ten administrative units; then into 129 production brigades; subsequently into production teams. Grains are the main crops, about equal rice and wheat; then corn, vegetables, and cotton; 3,400 cows producing 11 million kilos (24.2 million pounds) of milk a year. Each family has one or two pigs. There is a forestry program consisting mainly of fruit trees and grapevines. Many duck ponds—last year they sent 270,000 ducks to market. There are industries related to the commune; mills to process grains, and cotton, fourteen factories to process grapes for juice and wine. A total of 3,500 men and women work in the factories. Decisions about who works where are made at the brigade level—the first time on this trip I have been reminded that there is no personal choice about what one does or where one goes.

In the machine shop were big signs—Warmly Celebrate the Conclusion of the Eleventh Party Congress—and signs urging the workers to improve the factory output. There was no clapping to welcome us as there had been everywhere five years ago; but, as then, there were lots of men and women workers (more than seemed to me necessary) to do whatever they were doing—repairing machinery, I guess. H. thought they were just sitting around even more casually than before. I didn't notice the difference.

The irrigation system is excellent: a main canal with lots of water, and ditches in which it is carried to the fields. The water comes from a river nearby. They are putting the water into pipes so that it will be underground and they can use the land on top for more crops. In other words, they will use every inch.

We walked into a rice paddy, then visited Mr. Tung Thun in his own house, built last year by people who helped him for nothing and by others whom he paid, for what wasn't clear. Mr. Tung has his share of a community vegetable plot for his own vegetables. This used to be private, and he worked his share himself. Now they have machinery, so the entire plot is plowed and worked as a whole, and each person has a fair share of the produce.

They said that there are air raid shelters in this commune, though we didn't see any.

Mr. Tung's courtyard is shared by one or two other families. Vegetables are grown in a fairly good-sized garden, what we call a kitchen garden, and there is a big border of purple dahlias, the latter a big change from five years ago. We saw hardly any flowers then; every extra inch was used for growing food. Mr. Tung has ten chickens and two pigs for his family, which consists of six living with him. Obviously this family is content, well fed, and happy to have their own house, animals, and food. On the wall are pictures of wild animals, a departure from scenes from revolutionary ballets and movies and portraits of chairmen Mao and Hua. Harrison thinks this is significant.

There are no members of the People's Liberation Army in the Revolutionary Committee of this commune; there haven't been since 1971. In places we visited in 1972 there were always several, as I recall. At that time the Revolutionary Committees ran everything. We met with them at every school, university, factory, commune, and hospital we visited. Although this is the first commune we've seen this trip, the atmosphere seemed much less militant, more relaxed and easy. Young people come from the city to work here; in all, five thousand educated youth have been here. They stay two years. About fifteen hundred leave each year as others come.

Barefoot doctors are ordinary workers trained to take care of simple ailments, give acupuncture, give injections, and recognize when a patient needs more than simple treatment and should go to the hospital. At this commune clinic the barefoot doctor was a pretty girl about twenty years old with long pigtails and a pink shirt. She trained in the commune hospital for four months, then came to the clinic to do practical work. She goes back to the hospital for one month each year. She said she is never separated from her patients; she (and all doctors) go to their patients even out in the fields, to help and treat them. I think this is a big propaganda pitch, because the Chinese think our doctors are impersonal and not involved with their patients, which of course is true in many cases, especially in our big city hospitals.

I asked if she would like to study to become a real doctor, and she replied just what I knew she would say; "Only if my country wants me to and needs me in that capacity." And then she said she would want to come back to this, her commune, and serve these people. This is the first time I have heard that phrase. We have seen no buttons either, of Mao or "Serve the People." Last time almost everyone wore one.

There is a chart on the wall of the clinic with the names of young men of marriageable age who have not married. One was thirty-nine and had resisted so far. It is odd; they don't want people to marry young, but they want them married when they get to be about thirty. I guess it makes for a more stable society.

Another chart, under which I was sitting, lists all the women in that part of the commune who go to that clinic. It tells their age, what kind of contraceptive they "prefer," and how many children they have had. Under one woman's name there was a check in a different column from the others, and I asked what that meant. "She is beyond child-bearing age," was the answer. The lack of privacy is something I can never believe.

The ideal here in China, as anyone who has read anything about the subject knows, is for men to marry at age twenty-eight and girls at age twenty-five. Two children, five years apart, are recommended. I asked if women were made to have abortions if they became pregnant after having two children, and that answer also was what I expected. Abortion is available, but there is such a persuasive program of teaching that it is not necessary. A severe-looking woman is in charge of this program.

Although according to what we have been told the population of China is currently 900 million, up 100 million in five years, with this kind of program they are bound to spread knowledge of birth control and family planning. City girls who have been taught the ideal go to the countryside to help teach and influence the peasant girls. So eventually the birthrate should be slowed and maybe stabilized.

I don't believe that this is happening in India. I remember visiting a family-planning center near New Delhi several years ago, and they were having a terrible time persuading Indian women to use the loop, or IUD. The women refused to have male doctors; there was much supersitition; and I believe that that particular program was given up.

On our last trip here we visited a hospital to watch operations done with acupuncture anesthesia, and we saw and talked to several barefoot doctors. I don't know what we will be doing this time, but I hope it won't be all factories and political talk. I am terribly impressed at what China has done in caring for her people and would like to see more of it. An American surgeon who has just been here told me that the thing that impressed him the most was the delivery of health care. Everyone is included. If a man is sick and can't go to work, he doesn't just stay home; he goes to the barefoot doctor. So he gets the attention he needs. If he needs more than that doctor can give, he is sent to the hospital.

This American doctor said he thought the hospitals had suffered greatly from the Cultural Revolution. They really have lost ten years, he thinks. Cardiac and vascular surgery, for example, have made "great leaps forward," and China has not been able to keep up. Medical schools were closed, and there was no research into new medicines and techniques. But what they do know and have is distributed to everyone. He was also impressed that everyone is working or doing something. "No one is lonely," he said.

At three-thirty we went again to the Great Hall of the People to see Mr. Teng Hsiao-ping greet Mr. Vance and to hear the opening chit-chat. As Mr. Teng came down the line of journalists, he said, with a twinkle, "I have been reading what you have written—some of it is accurate, some is not." He noticed that I was standing behind some tall men and reached in to shake my hand. He is very small and solid, and toughness emanates from his sturdy little body. His face is smooth, and he certainly doesn't look his age—seventy-three.

This morning Mr. Mao and I were talking about this extraordinary man, who was a close friend and cohort of Chou En-lai from the time they went to Paris together as university students. He has been in and out of favor three or more times, the last and most conspicuous being during the end of the Gang's control, when they were criticizing Premier Chou so cruelly. I asked Mr. Mao how he could trust a man who had been in and out of favor so often. He replied, "Oh, because of that, we trust him more."

This in-and-out business is hard for me to understand. People are completely in one day and completely out the next. I don't understand how the Chinese powers of the moment expect us, or anyone, to accept this kind of maneuvering without questions.

24

(Since we have been home, a friend sent us a clipping from *Scientia Sinica*, and I quote: "Correction: In the article 'Devote Every Effort to Running Successfully Socialist Research Institutes of Science' [*Sci. Sin.* 19, no. 5], 'the arch unrepentant capitalist-roader in the Party Teng Hsiao-ping' should read 'Teng Hsiao-ping.'—The Editors.")

As they sat down, Mr. Teng asked Mr. Vance if he wanted to smoke. Vance said, "No, thanks." Teng then launched into a monologue about Yenan at the time that the Long March ended there in 1936. The Eighth Route Army had to grow their food and make their clothes because the peasants were so poor they had nothing to spare. Soldiers "had to use their own hands to feed and clothe themselves," he said, adding to the assembled delegates, "So now if any of you wish to enjoy the pleasure of smoking, you must use your own hands," meaning that they must pick up the cigarettes that were on the tables beside each man. Silly diplomatic chit-chat to fill up the time before serious talk began.

It is curious that the Chinese smoke so much. Neither of our interpreter friends, Yao Wei or Mr. Mao, smoke, but Chairman Mao was a heavy smoker, as was Chou En-lai. At all dinners and banquets everyone seems to smoke, and many people have cigarettes in their mouths constantly. Good cigarettes are expensive here, relatively more so than at home, but there are many brands of varying quality. Harrison thinks there is less smoking on the whole than on our last visit in 1972.

After that we went to a kindergarten. Mrs. Vance was

scheduled to go but decided not to. We thought she looked tired at the commune this morning. This kind of visit must be exhausting for her. I find what we do, just following on behind, very wearing, and she is on show every minute. We think she is lovely and doing a great job in her role.

This kindergarten must be for children of the elite—though there is not supposed to be such a thing—because it costs quite a lot, relatively speaking. It was set up in 1954 and has a staff of forty-six for two hundred children, three and a half to seven years old, which is when they start school. The staff takes turns staying at night. Children are divided into seven classes according to age, with three teachers to a class: two academics in charge of education and one in charge of their physical lives and their health. The academic teachers are graduates of the university. The parents are all workers, many in factories, some teachers. Parents leave their children Monday morning and pick them up Saturday afternoon. The union pays part of the cost. Children are taught from the beginning to love their leader, to love each other, and to love labor. They are taught by practical means; for instance, the children were taken to a recent parade celebrating the conclusion of the Eleventh Party Congress and told what it meant. I wonder what a three-year-old makes of that. Sometimes they go to the country at harvest time to do light labor in order to learn how much work it takes to grow vegetables, so that they will realize they must not waste food. They are also taught languages, dancing, and painting so that they will have some knowledge before going to primary school.

A great deal of attention is paid to health; they have good food, excercises, and sports. They have regular morning excercises, then run around the courtyard. They swim in summer, play ball in winter. They have regular physical checkups, injections, immunizations. Teachers have contact with parents about the children's health and behavior, and the parents are urged to tell the kindergarten how their children behave at home.

The children played a game of musical chairs. One child, acting as a policeman, stood in the middle directing the others with red and green stop signs. It is a good way to teach about traffic signals, but so far I have seen no sign of anyone paying attention to them in Peking. People walk across the streets any which way, and bicycles, while they go in the same direction as the trucks and cars, are all over the streets.

Four-and-a-half-year-olds are learning to count.

The whole school gave us a dance and recital. First was a dance celebrating the Eleventh Party Congress. I suppose tiny children don't pay much attention to the words and meaning, so it might as well be "Three Blind Mice" or "The Farmer in the Dell." Next was a Tibetan dance about a red flag that is handed down from one generation to the other. A third, "We will learn from Tachai" and "I will lead a plain life forever, my mother has mended my clothes." Fourth was about a model worker from Taching, the huge oil field in Manchuria. Tachai is the model agricultural area where good productive land has been built up on steep, erstwhile barren slopes.

Everything was done by hand. It is held up as the ideal. Taching is the same ideal industrially—"Learn from Taching," one hears constantly. On the wild, windy, treeless steppe there is now the biggest oil field in China, complete with housing, agriculture, schools, hospitals, and it is still growing. We are going there later on.

Next was a dance about picking apples. "We've come to the orchard to see our apples, they are so sweet, so red and delicious. Let's pick the best of them to give to our Chairman Hua," caroled the shrill little voices. A Mongolian dance was dedicated to Chairman Mao. "We are always thinking of you, our beloved Chairman Mao. You're the reddist thing in our hearts. We'll uphold the red banner and go forward forever." Another dance was performed by boys, "Learning from the Eighth Route Army." It was done with red-tasseled spears. Next, another song, "How Wise Our Chairman Hua Is, He Smashed the Four Pests."

In the last song the children built up the Tien An-Men gate using large painted blocks to represent parts of the gate. "How happy we are in the kindergarten, we are dancing and singing the whole day. We thank our Chairman Mao for giving us such a wonderful life. I love the chairman. The red sun is rising from the chairman," they sang.

At this kindergarten five of the staff are members of the Revolutionary Committee. Children are treated as children, they said. Teachers tell them stories, some political, some about agriculture, all commonsense stories. But also they now tell the old Chinese fairy tales, which hasn't always been the case.

Kindergartens I have seen in communist countries are much more regimented than those in the United States and the several in Japan that I visited just before coming here. In ours there seems to be very little discipline and no sense of the group. Children are free to paint the way they want, for instance, or to sit alone if they prefer, "to do their own thing." In Tokyo it was the same. No one was asked to greet a visitor or to perform for her; there was no group feeling. Children were every which way, whiling away the time rather than being taught.

In China the kindergarten is the entity, the children each a part but acting as a whole. They clap or sing hello, they give dances and recitations, they illustrate their games, which always teach a moral or a worthwhile fact. I can't say that either way produces happier or better children, but I have never seen a child cry or appear unhappy in China. They are always busy doing something organized, and acting as if they liked it.

The staff here (and everyone we have talked to so far, in fact) seems gung ho for the Eleventh Party Congress and the party line of the moment.

From the kindergarten we were whisked to the Summer Palace, where Mr. Teng was to entertain the Vance group at a banquet. First there was a boat ride on three gorgeous painted barges. Mr. and Mrs. Vance, Mr. Teng, and all the most important people were on one barge, the journalists and interpreters on the other two. Slowly we went around the lake, floating luxuriously, drinking the ever-present orange pop and tea, nibbling peanuts, almonds, and those crispy rice wafers. It is incredible the way the communists "lay it on"—on a par with the Japanese.

It was terribly pretty out on the lake, and no one else was there. The hoi polloi had been removed. The last time we were at the Summer Palace with the Dudmans in 1972, the lake was solid with people in rowboats, and hundreds of Chinese were enjoying the now-public park. Tonight we enjoyed it as the emperors must have.

After about a half-hour boat ride we disembarked at the restaurant. The "royal party" sat in splendor at the banquet table, and we were allowed to watch them from an adjoining room and take pictures for a few minutes. Then all the correspondents and their interpreters and Chinese companions, with Mr. Ma of the Press Department of the Foreign Office, retired to a common dining room, where we had the same food and drink as the others but in an everyday setting. An absolutely fabulous meal. Course after course of divine-looking and divine-tasting delicacies. Someone asked Mr. Ma how such a meal compared with an everyday meal for a regular family, and he said, "No one eats like this." The usual meal is rice and vegetables and maybe a little bit of meat or fish. Mr. Mao, our companion, eats porridge for breakfast. Fox Butterfield had Chinese soup at breakfast every day at the hotel, but no rice. Also, Mr. Mao said the food at the Summer Palace is superior to that in the Great Hall of the People, a statement with which we agree.

Thursday, August 25

TODAY WE WENT to the Spare-Time Sports School, lunched with Mr. Chien Chi-seng, head of the Information Department, Mr. Ma's boss, then to the Great Hall to see Chairman Hua meet Cyrus Vance.

We visited the sports school with Mrs. Vance. The school teaches sports, dancing, and exercises similar to the Yoga way of stretching and balancing. Beginning at five years old, children go there for three hours a day in summer (I don't know how often in winter, but I suppose in whatever spare time they have). Boys learn the typical shadow boxing, acrobatics, and traditional manly arts; girls take dancing, a mixture of ballet and excercising that they use in their ballets, and other more violent dances and acts with swords. I felt the same as I did when I saw the kindergarten: Any society that can train their children to excel like this can do anything. When we were in Shanghai in 1972, we visited a Children's Palace, to which schoolchildren go two afternoons a week to learn a skill—playing a musical instrument, leading a chorus, making paper cutouts, model boat and plane building, painting, sewing, even acupuncture and herbal medicine. I said to Harrison at that time, "It's like a slot machine—put in a child and get out an expert."

All these children seem proud, happy, skilled, and dedicated to the government and society that makes them feel this way.

Mrs. Vance played Ping-Pong and did everything she was supposed to do and looked pretty and natural.

Mr. Chien Chi-seng entertained us for lunch in a private dining room in our hotel. Present were H. and me, Mr. Ma, Mr. Mao, Mr. Liu (also in the Press Department—the one who chewed out Fox Butterfield), and another man. Harrison is wonderful the way he can talk to all these people, both seriously and in fun. Mr. Chien said to him, "Now that you are no longer with the *New York Times*, we don't like their attitude toward China." The ads from Taiwan are especially irritating to them, but there was an editorial not long ago suggesting that relations between China and the United States should be normalized, and no one at lunch seemed to be aware of it.

It was an interesting discussion of the Soviet Union, the United States, China, President Carter, Mr. Brzezinski and more. A real feast, too. We eat too much here.

Later we went to the Great Hall and watched Chairman Hua meet Mr. Vance. Chairman Hua looks a little like Chairman Mao. He is the same shape and seems the same size, though I never actually saw Chairman Mao. When we first saw pictures of Mao, he was already a hero, so we were conditioned to that fact. If he hadn't been the leader of the Revolution, he might have looked to us like an everyday Chinese. That is how Chairman Hua looks to me—just an ordinary man—not like Mao (or Professor Higgins in *My Fair Lady*) and certainly not the equal of Chou En-lai in worldliness, sophistication, and warmth. He obviously has strength and character and daring, and the backing and support of many Chinese, so maybe it will show in him gradually. It is probably too soon for him to look like a great leader.

As on the two previous days, we rushed into the conference room and watched the dignitaries sit down and talk pleasantries for the newsreels. Chairman Hua said that the Shanghai Communiqué must be the basis for any agreement. Mr. Vance nodded and smiled, and we left.

Tonight Mr. and Mrs. Vance gave a dinner at the Great Hall for the Chinese. It was the same kind of evening as when Huang Hua gave the first dinner—a banquet, speeches, and a toast at the end, and nothing said. We sat at a table with Mr. Ma, of the Press Office; Fox Butterfield; the Rick Smith who is here, not the *New York Times* Hedrick Smith, the *Voice of America* young man who kept falling asleep (he had been up most of the night sending messages); and Mr. Mao, next to me. It was fun but not exciting, and Mr. Mao is right. The food is nowhere near as good as at the Summer Palace.

Mr. Vance had a press conference at this hotel afterward, but I don't see why. He wasn't going to let anything out (if there is anything to let out, which doesn't seem likely) and got very annoyed at Bernard Kalb for asking questions, which after all is his job. Vance is in an awkward position. Carter doesn't seem to be aware of China and is dragging his feet on the whole issue, and Vance is sent over here to do what? It seems to me that nothing happened and nothing has changed. I wonder why he was sent at all. It must have cost a pretty penny.

Friday, August 26

I DIDN'T GO to breakfast because I've been eating too
much—had fruit and coffee in our room. At 8:30 we
drove, again in procession, to the airport to watch the
Vance party leave. All the journalists except those from
Hong Kong left with him on the plane. The latter are
staying until tomorrow. We made the one-hour trip out
there in our separate cars with our own interpreters, and
we drove back with many empty cars in the same orderly
way.

We are now relegated to a smaller dining room in the
back, across from the private room where we had lunch
with Mr. Chien. We still sit at a round table with eight or
more places, and there are two more tables for four. So
funny. The dining room where we had been eating is now
full of Japanese; the room they ate in is being scrubbed,
and the Yugoslavs, who are beginning to arrive because
Tito is coming here next week, seem to be eating in the
other big dining room called the Western Dining Room,
to the left of the front door. I don't know where the
Chinese eat, but often I see several coming down the

stairs at mealtimes, so maybe they eat up on the next floor.

We sat with Jack Reynolds, of NBC, at lunch. He lives in Hong Kong and has a Chinese wife. He has been here six times and covered the private trip Nixon made after he resigned from the presidency. Jack told us that during that visit he was filming on a Peking street, and a large crowd gathered to watch. As people came closer and closer, the Chinese who were with him became hysterical and asked him to stop filming. He suggested they tell the crowd he was making a film because of Nixon's visit. The Chinese refused to do this and cried out, "Stop. Look what you're doing. It's your fault, the masses are out of control." He said the crowd wasn't angry or threatening, only curious, but his Chinese companions were clearly afraid of a mob. Chiang Ching was still around at that time. She received Nixon, and I guess there was reason for some people to be uptight and nervous.

After a short rest we went to a steel and iron complex. The blast furnaces were not going, but three convertors were. After walking around the plant, which didn't mean much to me except that everything was black, we climbed up to a glass-enclosed room opposite the convertors and watched while pig iron, carbon, and other elements were put into large vats and heated until everything melted together to make steel. Even from an enclosed area and at a distance of at least seventy-five feet it felt hot. I don't see how people can stand working as close to the convertors as they have to, no matter how they are protected.

When the contents are melted, the vats are tipped, and the flaming liquid is poured into other containers, sparks and fire spurting all over, and taken to machines that turn it into different forms. It was exciting, in a terrifying way, but I was happy to get out of that hot booth.

It is interesting that only in communist countries do I go to steel mills, factories, and, next week, oil fields. Maybe I should make this kind of a trip in my own country some day, but I can't imagine going to another steel mill, no matter where it is.

For our briefing it was a relief to sit in a huge room and drink tea with the two head men. Armchairs and sofas slip-covered in cotton were grouped around tables in the usual way for meetings, but at the other end of the room elaborate black inlaid lacquer tables and chairs stood against the wall. They must have belonged to the warlord who built this complex in 1919. It came into the hands of the people in 1948, and in 1950–52 it produced more than twice as much iron was was produced in the thirty years previous, they told us.

As was the case all over China, this factory was helped by the Soviets until 1960, when differences in ideology caused them to leave. There had been eight Russian experts here to teach and advise, and when they left, they took even the blueprints with them. So the Chinese had to "make do" and "innovate," two phrases we heard every day on our last visit. The workers commented that the Soviet equipment was big, clumsy, and heavy, the head men said.

They talked a lot about the bad effects of Liu Shao-chi,

Lin Piao, and the Gang of Four and told us that the smashing of the Gang had had a very beneficial effect on the workers. There are sixty thousand workers here now; ten thousand in the mines, ten thousand for capital construction, and forty thousand and staff engaged in production. I asked where the workers come from and if they choose to work here. The answer was that they are sent by the Workers' Bureau. The factory tells when and how many workers it needs, and they are sent along. Choice? Not really. They are paid sixty yuan a month, about thirty dollars. A one-room courtyard house rents for two yuan a month, and a new apartment is three or four. Rent includes water and electricity. Leaders' wages, including the engineers' and the main directors', are about double those of the workers. Approximately 20 percent of workers are women, and while ordinarily they do the same work as men and earn as much, during pregnancy they are transferred to lighter work. Nursery and kindergarten cost four yuan a month, ten for children over four years old. Primary school is two yuan twice a year, to cover the cost of books. High school is about four yuan a term. They were amazed to learn that public education is free in the United States.

They know so little about us and our system and government, and I wonder if they really believe or take in what we tell them. A friend of ours recently visited an English-language class in Nanking University. The students were learning English from a workbook that, she noticed, was made up of primarily negative statements and quotations about Blacks in the United States (that they had to sit at the back of the bus, had to use separate toilets) as well as propaganda about how the capitalists in America have the most advanced technology in the world and the Blacks must overthrow the capitalists and get control of it themselves. They asked her if it was possible for Blacks to get an education in the United States. They had heard it was not. She talked to them for a long time but wasn't at all sure she had convinced them that everybody goes to school, in fact has to. So often the young Chinese we meet seem to have their minds made up and are not interested in hearing a new idea if it doesn't fit in with what they have been taught. Communism is all good; capitalism is all wrong.

This evening Frank Coe and his wife, Ruth, took us out to dinner. He was in the Treasury Department in Washington and was a victim of the McCarthy era. They came here in the 1950s. He doesn't speak Chinese, said he was over fifty when he arrived here and just couldn't learn. But Ruth does and seems to manage everything easily. He is connected to the Institute for Higher Economic Studies, and she works for Hsinhua, the Chinese news agency.

They took us to the Hsin Chiao Hotel, where many embassy people go to eat, and we had caviar, soup, and ice cream—a relief from all the banquets, and yet a banquet in its own way for caviar lovers. This caviar is Chinese. It comes from their own rivers. We had three orders among us, and each order was a huge mound of the fantastic delicacy served with little pieces of toast, egg, and onion. (At the Friendship Store we found it for sale in jars of almost a pound for fourteen dollars!!! At home it is nearly one hundred dollars for one-half pound.)

Afterward we went back to their house, which is part of what used to be one rich man's house. It consisted of many large courtyards and complexes of rooms. We walked through the gate off a tiny *hu tung* (old Chinese street) near the Drum Tower and into a rectangular courtyard with three doors opening off it, then through the right-hand door into a very pretty courtyard with trees and a fountain in the middle. From that we stepped into a marvelous house that seemed to go on for miles, with old Chinese furniture and wonderful carved woodwork.

Before Liberation this is the way all the "foreign friends" lived, except that they would have had a whole elegant house to themselves, with all the courtyards—no sharing in those days. And as many servants as they wanted for practically nothing.

It was terribly hot—in the nineties—and I wondered if they ever use fans. It is clear why the Chinese are always sitting on the sidewalks and in the streets in the evenings if their houses are all as hot as this was, and they're probably worse because they are smaller and more crowded.

We had coffee and beer and talked for a while about what is happening in China and how baffling many things are even to people who live here. Harrison said he could have stayed all night talking to Frank, but I was falling asleep. He will just have to go by himself another time—I can't keep going the way he can. This is a very tiring country to be in under the circumstances we're under, and I am exhausted a lot of the time. I don't sleep well; it is so noisy. I don't mind the heat half as much as the constant noise of car horns, roaring traffic, screaming propaganda. Even in mills and factories, where it is noisy enough normally, those shrill voices scream out advice for working harder to improve production.

Saturday, August 27

OUR HONG KONG friends left today after breakfast, and now we sit alone at a table set for two in the small dining room in the back.

In the morning we went to a blanket and fabric factory. I have never been to this kind of factory before and was fascinated at all the steps the wool goes through, including many washings in suds and very hot water. Having been brought up to wash my sweaters in cold water, I was surprised at the heat, but was told it is common treatment in all wool factories.

There are six workshops for sorting, washing, spinning, combing, weaving, and finishing products and manufacturing plush, which is popular for linings for coats in winter. "Old people like it because it is light in weight and cheaper and more practical than fur," we were told. A total of 2,800 workers, half of them women, work in three shifts around the clock, 1,500 on the day shift, 700 and 600 respectively, on the other two. The average wage is fifty-seven yuan a month. All are production workers; there is no commune attached to this factory. There are 6,500 spindles and 150 looms, carding machines, etc. Forty percent of the machinery is imported from Japan. The main products are wool, corduroy, plush, artificial fibers, and blankets (500,000 of pure wool, 100,000 synthetic a year.) They use goat hair, camel hair, pure wool, synthetics, and mixtures. Every year there is an increase of 8 percent in production, they said. Designing groups go to the countryside to find out what kind of patterns people like the most, and every year there are new designs, more variety than in other countries, they think. One half of the blankets and 40 percent of the material are for export to more than thirty countries. Much goes to Hong Kong for reexport to the Middle East, Africa, Japan, and Syria. I couldn't figure out which thirty countries they meant.

They have nurseries and kindergartens and a clinic for the workers but no schools. There is some housing, but many people live in the city and commute by bus or bicycle (about one-half hour).

The most interesting thing is that the head man, Mr. Wang Chen, who came here in 1964 to design, is a graduate of the Peking Arts and Crafts Institute. He is vice-chairman of the Revolutionary Committee, but his role is artistic; he didn't seem to know much about production and figures. Mr. Lin, the head of the technology department, supplied those details. They both said that the Gang of Four hadn't bothered them much.

After lunch and a rest we visited the air raid shelters. Last time we were not taken to an air raid shelter or allowed to see the subway that was being built, though we asked several times to do so. But now most important foreigners and newspapermen are taken on a tour of the shelters, if not the subway. Rather than shelters, they are really tunnels under the city designed to get people to the suburbs in the event of a nuclear attack. They are only just wide enough for two people to walk abreast, and I can't think of anything more terrifying than someone falling in such a narrow place with thousands of people running behind, all trying to escape a nuclear bomb. Many would be trampled; it would be a double catastrophe.

This system under Peking was built in 1970 mainly by retired workers, housewives, and people from factories, the average age being fifty. The section we were in is 980 meters (1,072 yards) long altogether, and there are more than ninety entrances all over the city. We entered from a clothing store, where the steps were hidden under a sliding floor behind a counter. It is a veritable labyrinth of tunnels all running into and connecting with each other and leading out of the city. Occasionally there is a turnout, a space so that someone could get out of line in an emergency if the emergency occurred at that place, and there are toilets, generators, canteens, air purifiers. (How is nuclear fallout purified or sifted so that you can breathe immediately?) They told us there is a primary school down at a lower level, grain storage rooms, workshops, a hospital, broadcasting system, and theater. We wonder if there is not another set of tunnels farther down that are wider and if what we saw is the first shelter they made and the one they show to visitors. There is terrible condensation, but they say it occurs only at this time of year.

We walked for about a mile in the cool tunnels and came out in a different place. From there we took a ride on the subway. It is clean and neat, not crowded at all on the platforms, though the trains were full. As every visitor has observed, all Chinese people—both men and women—get up and offer their seats to foreigners, the same as in Russia. Always embarrassing.

We dined tonight with Huang Hua, our friend from the United Nations, and now foreign minister, and his wife Madame Ho, at a restaurant very near to our hotel. We made this trip in a taxi; number sixty-one is gone, along with all the correspondents and the Vance entourage. The restaurant is a large courtyard house that must have belonged to a millionaire, and we had a Szechuan meal because that is where Madame Ho comes from. Generally Szechuan food is spicy and hot, but in deference to us it was milder than usual. Even so, some dishes were terribly hot, and I had to gulp water between mouthfuls. Though it is delicious, that type of Chinese food has never appealed to me as much as most others; there are not enough green vegetables.

As is the custom, Harrison sat on Huang Hua's right, and I sat at the other end of the table, on Madame Ho's right. Mr. Mao was on my other side. Guests included Mr. Tang, who is in the United Nations Secretariat and has been to our house in New York; Mr. Ma, Mr. Chien, who had us for lunch the other day, and a Mr. Ping.

45

Harrison thought the foreign minister was weary and depressed, obviously over the lack of any accomplishment during the Vance visit. He didn't talk about that, but did about the Gang of Four. I was reminded of dinners we had had together in New York and how relaxed and what fun they were. Harrison kept trying to cheer him up, talking and asking about people we know, among them Chiao Kuang-hua, former foreign minister. He is still at the Ministry, but with no responsibility, and is "studying his mistakes." Harrison asked, "And do you think he is a good student?" which made them all laugh and broke the gloom a bit.

Madame Ho wears no makeup, but her hair is soft and wavy, and she is very pretty. She wears gray trousers and short-sleeved shirts—the other night she wore a pink one, and tonight's was a muted plaid design in tan cotton. She is an extremely attractive, warm, and friendly woman, sophisticated in a simple, natural way as only the Chinese are. It was nice of them to have us for dinner when they are tired from the diplomatic visit and probably fed up with the United States.

Sunday, August 28

THIS MORNING Yao Wei, our interpreter and companion of 1972, came to see us. Though Harrison is usually as reserved as the Chinese, he hugged Yao Wei. I was more Chinese and just shook hands. He looks wonderful. He told us that he had spent about a year at a May Seventh school doing physical labor in the countryside and was enthusiastic about the experience. He looks stronger and more filled out than I remember him.

We have been told that some people chose to go to May Seventh schools during the last few years of the Gang's control, just to be out of the way and doing something no one could find fault with. I don't know if that was the case with Yao Wei, or if he was ordered to go. Whichever it was, he enjoyed it and obviously is in much-improved physical shape.

He said he isn't doing much interpreting now, feels it is very tiring and that he is too old. He is forty-six. He will be with the American publishers and editors while they are in Peking next week but will not travel with them. That is for younger interpreters, he said. He does some translations. We talked about the other Americans he has been with in the past, among them Robert Rodale, editor of *Organic Gardening and Farming*, whom I admire greatly, and Joseph Alsop, the writer. The latter is one of the lucky Americans who can compare the old China with the new. He was with the United States forces over here during World War II and spent some time in a Japanese prison camp. (Since this was written, Yao Wei has been promoted to the Foreign Office.)

We lunched with Ross and Judy Munro. He is the reporter for the *Toronto Globe and Mail* (he has since been expelled by the Chinese.) Mr. Gerson, from the British Embassy, and his attractive wife were also there. I wore a skirt and a necklace, and we had white wine—like at home.

The Gersons have been to Ulan Bator in Outer Mongolia, so that gave us an immediate bond. They told us about a Mongol driver at the British Embassy there who kept an eye on the other Mongols who were working at the embassy, for the Mongolian government. His fellow Mongols found out he was spying on them and one day put acid in his boots, so that when he put them on, his feet nearly burned off. Mrs. Gerson said she couldn't imagine what he was doing, jumping around and screaming. She thought it was because he didn't want to drive her to some place she wanted to go.

They also told us a horror story about a Rumanian girl who had a terrible pain in her stomach. She went to the Russian hospital because it is supposed to be very good, but they refused to help her because she was not Russian.

So she went to the Mongolian hospital, where they tied her down on the operating table and took out her appendix without any anesthetic, not even an aspirin. She has a long, ugly scar to boot. (I'm glad I wasn't sick when we were there in 1969.)

Mrs. Munro told me that there is a black market in coupons here. Coupons are necessary for oil, cotton, and several other products, and there is some undercover wheeling and dealing. She also said that in Canton, people were seen selling diamond watches on the street and that Chinese people were buying them but that nothing like that had been noticed in Peking.

She showed me some reproductions of the peasant paintings of Huhsien, which are being shown in various cities in the United States. They are simple, primitive, colorful, and attractive paintings of everyday life in the villages, fields, factories—much like our early American paintings and especially like those of Grandma Moses. They are done by peasants in their spare time and are described by the Chinese People's Association for Friendship with Foreign Countries as "painted by the hands of those who work with hoes the year round. Full of revolutionary poetry and militant zeal, these paintings belong to a new form of art." A further comment by the same group: "The fact that Chinese peasants have taken the paintbrush in hand and entered the arena of art shows that the working people are not only creators of material wealth but also creators of intellectual wealth and masters of culture and art. This is of far-reaching significance to the abolition of the distinction between manual workers and brain workers."

These paintings are far more appealing than most of what we saw in an exhibit here in 1972. With few exceptions, those pictures were similar to what the Soviets call Socialist Realist painting—scenes of coal mines; steel mills; factories; soldiers; Chairman Mao reading, teaching, leading discussions, marching with troops. The peasant paintings reflect the life of the workers, as Mao said all art should, but they are small and delicate and personal compared with the earlier sweeping canvases of militant communist propaganda.

Mrs. Munro is a photographer, so she has work of her own. It is easier in a place and situation like this for a woman to have a profession or interest separate from her husband's that she can pursue. Most of the foreign women I have met in China seem to begin by studying Chinese, but when they get so that they can manage in stores and in the street, they stop. They say that Chinese is so difficult that it would take years of intensive study to be able really to talk to a Chinese. That makes our friend Inge Miller even more remarkable than I already think she is. She had been studying Chinese for one year when I introduced her to Madame Ho in New York. After hearing Inge say a few words, Madame Ho said, "I can't believe my ears." Her pronunciation was perfect, and she spoke with ease.

After dinner we called on Rewi Alley, the eighty-year-old New Zealander who has lived in China since 1926. His beautiful apartment is in the former Italian Embassy compound; the main building is now the headquarters for the China Friendship Society, in which both **Mr. Mao** and Yao Wei work. When we drove through the gate, I had the most intense feeling of déjà vu, not for the main embassy but for the building on the right and the arrangement of the gardens. I know I have been there before.

We drove first to the big building, but it was closed, and no one was in sight. It is a handsome building, and I couldn't help but imagine how busy and noisy and what fun it must have been when the Italians were in residence there. Now they must be in some nondescript residence inside the embassy compound. Back at the front gate Harrison found an office where he had to register who we were and whom we wanted to visit; then we were permitted to go to the first door.

It was wonderful inside, beautiful dark woodwork, millions of books, beautiful scrolls on the walls—a mixture of Chinese and ordinary furniture. Anna Louise Strong, the American radical who was involved with both the Russian and the Chinese revolutionary movements, used to live in this apartment, and Mr. Alley lived upstairs. They took their meals together, on the porch when the pomegranates were in bloom. Such a delicate touch for such a violent, strange communist woman. (Later, when we dined with Madame Soong, Sun Yat-Sen's widow, and Rewi Alley was present, Madame Soong said with some feeling that "they had breakfast together for eleven years.") Rewi said it was always interesting if sometimes wild. He moved down to her apartment when she died.

Rewi Alley was a sheep farmer in New Zealand when he was young, but the wool market went to pot, and anyone in the wool business lost everything. He went to sea, stopped off at Shanghai for a few days to see something of China, and has never been home except for a visit. He is roly-poly, white-haired, and very soft-spoken, and has a childlike quality that people are apt to have when they are steeped in this society. Perhaps that isn't the right way to describe it; some of the foreign residents here seem disillusioned and bitter. I gather the several women foreigners who have been such friends of China have had neither of these qualities, and the Chinese we know are anything but innocent. Yet they do have a simplicity and directness that are disarming.

Anyway, he is a sweet man. Even at eighty he travels in China for six months of every year, and there is hardly an inch of this huge country that he has not seen. He takes pictures and writes articles for *Eastern Horizon, China Reconstructs*, and other periodicals, and he is also a poet. He used to have a school for young Chinese boys, and many of his old students come to see him; many had been there today.

We had tea and coffee and delicious candied apricots and nuts while he told us stories and some of his experiences. He told us about a man connected to the Gang of Four, a scientist, who had had a warning of the earthquake in Lanshan a year ago and didn't inform the people where it hit worst. (We heard this story many times during our visit.) When we left, he walked with us to the door and kissed me good-bye—very un-Chinese.

Monday, August 29

THIS MORNING we went to the Institute for Minorities and spent nearly three hours there. The head is a genial old guy who is an anthropologist. He studied in London in the 1930s and was in the United States in 1943–44 at Harvard and the University of Chicago.

This institute was started after Liberation—they had their first students in 1951. The object is to study the history, language, and culture of the minorities so that their way of life can be preserved. Of all the people in China 94 percent are Han people, who are regarded as the real Chinese. The other 6 percent is made up of fifty-four minorities. Before Liberation there were six national languages and countless dialects; many minorities still have no written system because they cannot find a common language among themselves. The government is trying to make Mandarin (or Peking) Chinese the language for everyone, but this will take time. (We noticed on our last trip that our interpreter often had trouble understanding what was said when we were far away from Peking.)

All this makes translation a big problem. The institute prints newspapers in many languages—we saw at least fifteen in all sorts of lettering: Cyrillic, Latin, Sanskrit, Turkic, and many more. The fifth volume of Mao's works has just been translated into five languages: Tibetan, Mongol, Uighur, Korean, and Kazak.

There is a preparatory course here that enables minorities to go to other universities. As they say, "We become a bridge, from here one can go to other universities, walk on two legs." If a minority member is studying his own literature, he must also study Han literature. They have a very active music and dance department. Our host said they have learned from the minorities that "the real source of art is the people." Living folk art, they call it. In the past, Han art and dance was specialized for performance on the stage; now real living art is shown. Chiang Ching, who was the cultural head of the People's Republic of China until Mao died, did not allow folk music and dance to be performed, pronouncing it vulgar. Now a professional group of dancers and singers of this kind of music and dance has been trained here.

There are two thousand students here now. At other times there have been as many as three thousand. In all, fifteen thousand have graduated since the institute started. There are more than one thousand workers altogether, six hundred of them teachers. Students come from all over, so there are many different calendars to reckon with. For instance, many New Years are celebrated besides the Chinese New Year. Everything is

free; students are supplied with pocket money, clothes, and special food. (Moslems don't eat pork, the basic meat of China.) They can wear their national costume if they want to, but many say they are too hot. That's what Japanese ladies have told me about kimonos.

Besides academic students, men and women from the minorities come here to be trained as party workers, or cadres, as they call them. When ready they are sent back to their villages to work with the people, to help them raise their standard of living, to teach in schools, to help in factories, to teach the way of life of the Chinese Communist Party.

Chinese cadres also study the language and history of a minority region and go out to those areas to live and work.

With all this helping, which is also indoctrination, I don't see how the minorities can preserve their culture except in the arts and for show. Their daily life is bound to become more and more Chinese. When we go to Inner Mongolia, we can see for ourselves.

At three-thirty we whirled once more to the Great Hall of the People to meet with Mr. Li Hsien-nien, third vice-chairman of the People's Republic of China. He greeted us just the way the big shots are greeted; we had our pictures taken and walked to the inner room and had tea and a talk for about one and a half hours. Present besides Mr. Li and Harrison and me were Mr. Ma, Nancy Tang (not an interpreter anymore but one of the chief deputies of the Foreign Office), Mr. Chien, Mr. Mao, Mr. Li from the Press Office. Behind the vice-chairman sat Mrs. Hsih

Yen-hua, the lovely interpreter who came to our house in New York when Huang Hua came for dinner a few years ago. Three women sat farther away, near a door. Harrison thought that perhaps they were a doctor and nurses—Vice-Chairman Li has a bad cough, is a very unhealthy color, and smokes a lot, as so many Chinese do. In the middle of the interview a cup of something special was brought to him, and he drank it down immediately as if it were medicine. But the three women were newspaper people, according to Mr. Mao.

Vice-Chairman Li looked cross and scary to me, but when he smiled or laughed, he became friendly and human. He obviously warmed to Harrison; he held his hand in both of his for quite a while when we said good-bye. Quite a few Chinese do this.

Mr. Li opened the conversation by saying, "I understand you know the Soviet Union well. You have written a book about war with Russia, you mentioned the truth. The Soviet Union won't let you in." So many of our interviews in 1972 began like that. Because he is a Russian specialist, the Chinese really struggled to get what they could out of him.

They discussed the Soviet threat. Mr. Li said that the Russian focus and three fourths of their strategic arms are concentrated in Europe, the Middle East, and Africa. "Who will be bitten first by the Polar Bear?" he asked. "Probably not China," he added. The Chinese think the United States is on the defensive, talking about détente, appeasing the Soviet Union, trying to defend its vested interests, while the Soviet Union is expanding in a big way.

He said, "Daily talk about détente and peace is like smoking opium; people drugged won't be prepared." He said this to Mr. Hamilton of the *London Times*, and the Soviets wrote a particular article attacking him. Mr. Li said, "I think it's good for them to attack me. If they didn't, it would mean I made mistakes. If you don't accuse them and they don't accuse you, it means you wallow in the same mire."

He said, "We will not fire the first shot. China wants genuine peace, not sham peace. Why should we want war? We are not rich. We have enough to do at home. But we'll expose those who really want war or are proposing sham peace."

There has been a blast of accusations hurled at China from the Soviet Union since the Eleventh Party Congress, calling the Chinese communist bandits, vagabonds, renegades, and traitors. He mentioned that they were also called these names by Chiang Kai-shek. Harrison remembered that Chiang Kai-shek had called Mao "the red bandit," and Mr. Li said, "That was the most polite term."

There are one million Russian troops on the Chinese border, but even two million would not be enough to attack China. Harrison asked, "Even if they use nuclear weapons?" Mr. Li replied, "We are not afraid of nuclear weapons; we don't believe they will level China, it's too big." He also said that those troops are really directed at Japan and the United States.

They talked a lot about the Gang of Four. Just as the Cultural Revolution was the main thing we tried to understand five years ago, this time it is the Gang of Four. How did they become so powerful when they were so close to Mao? What was the extent of the damage to industry and how long did it take, or will it take, to make up? What happened to the Gang; where are they?

Mr. Li said, "It is natural for our foreign friends to ask these questions." He went on to say that in 1966 Liu Shao-chi had become the worst reactionary in the party (he was the first man Mao chose to be his successor). The Gang pretended they were against Liu Shao-chi, though in reality they were in collusion with him. After he was out, in Chairman Li's words, they continued "to fish in troubled waters and seize power," ending up controlling the mass media, *China Daily*, Hsinhua, the journal *Red Flag*.

Mao, though old and ill, understood what the Gang was up to and criticized them many times, in 1971, 1974, and especially severely in 1975. He said then that the problem of the Gang must be settled, but he didn't have time to do so. But he made the best arrangement for after his death by appointing his "good student" Hua to be first vice-chairman, the first and only time he had ever had a first vice-chairman. Hua showed his strength by smashing the Gang only a month after Mao died, before they could seize control of the country. He was able to do this because he had the support of vast members of the People's Liberation Army and of the people.

As for the damage inflicted on industry by the Gang, Mr. Li said it was good we were going to visit Hangchow, where workers were influenced ideologically by the

Gang, a lot of fighting took place in the factories, and production came to a standstill. There is still a tiny handful of diehards; it is imperative to clean them out. It will take one or two years, maybe longer in some places, to restore production to previous levels.

There was very little upheaval in the Taching oil fields. The cadres and workers there resisted the Gang.

In the schools and universities the students have settled down to study, and teachers and scientific workers are in high spirits, Mr. Li said. There must be revolutionary education, but not the same as the Gang wanted. They were against the "Stinking Nine"—landlords, rich peasants, counterrevolutionaries, bad elements, rightists, renegades and traitors, special agents, capitalists and nine, intellectuals. He said number nine (intellectuals) should not be dispensed with and quoted Mao's saying, "Let one hundred schools of thought contend." I don't get what he means.

Harrison asked what was their method of dealing with the Gang, and Mr. Li answered, "We don't kill them; we let them live, and we feed them." He said Stalin was a great Marxist-Leninist, but he liked to kill people. "He was right to kill some, but he killed too many. Mao said we shouldn't kill—deprive them of all their political rights, expel them forever from the party and all posts inside and outside the party. It is not good for them to be at large."

H. asked what happened to Liu Shao-chi? Mr. Li answered, "He is idle, well advanced in years." H. said, "He's alive?" Mr. Li said, "How do you view the international situation?" H. replied, "Mr. Li is in a better position to answer that," but Harrison made no bones about believing that the United States should somehow resolve the Taiwan problem. Mr. Li said that obviously "President Carter hasn't made up his mind yet; he is reluctant to give up his old friend Taiwan. The Chinese people are quite unhappy."

He said the *New York Times* is unfriendly to China; they gave so much space to the pilot from the Chinese Air Force who fled to Taiwan. Why was it worthwhile to go into such detail about one person out of all the Chinese people? Harrison said there had been an editorial recently supporting immediate action to carry out the Shanghai Communiqué. Mr. Li had not seen that (neither had any Chinese we spoke to on this trip) and didn't seem convinced. He said he understood Mr. Sulzberger, publisher of the *New York Times*, was coming to China with a group of publishers and editors and added that "it is quite all right for them to come and exchange views with us."

Harrison asked about the population. Mr. Li said he didn't know the accurate number; he thinks it's about 800 million, but the economics department says it is more. "But they exaggerate." The birthrate is reduced, he said, especially in the cities. China makes sustained efforts to promote medical health conditions and technology, and basically even rural populations listen to the advice. Only old ladies don't agree, he said. "They always want to have more grandchildren, so what can you do about it?" But he felt the grandmothers would see the benefit of family planning before too long. Now the number of

60

primary-school students is reduced each year so that there are enough classrooms in the cities. Students can study all day instead of some in the morning and the rest in the afternoon. An Englishman suggested to him that by promoting planned parenthood they would not have enough labor. Mr. Li said, "We will never have that problem."

He mentioned that James Schlesinger, who was in China last year when Mao died, had gone to the Sino-Soviet border. H. said, "I'd like to do that myself." Mr. Li responded, "I wonder if it's the proper season; it takes a long time." H. said, "I have the time if the facilities are available." Laughter followed that, and Mr. Li said, "You are going to the border area in Mongolia." And that was that. "Border area" is not the border.

Mr. Li asked Harrison if he had read Chairman Hua's report on the Eleventh Party Congress, and H. replied yes, he'd read it all and that it was very thick, which made Mr. Li laugh. He talked about the congress being the congress of unity and victory and of all the difficulties and shocks the Chinese have suffered in the last year and a half, the deaths of Chou En-lai and Mao, the earthquakes, especially the losses in Lanshan, the city 120 miles from Peking where steel mills and coal mines were virtually destroyed. Restoration work is going on pretty fast, but it will take time to restore all the worker's houses. These three major events, deaths of old party leaders, earthquakes, and disruption by the Gang made it a hard time for the Chinese people and their government.

He said that the country is still poor, but comparing

the present level with what it was under Chiang Kai-shek, they have made enormous advances. People used to die unnatural deaths from disease, starvation, and cold. It was of no consequence to their leader. Now they have enough to eat and enough to wear. In years of disaster they have some reserves. The steel industry was miniscule under Chiang Kai-shek, he said, as were coal, textiles, watches. There was no petrochemical industry, no machine building, only machine repair shops to serve foreign business. And all industry was owned either by foreigners or by four big Chinese families.

Mr. Li said it would be cooler in Taching; H. replied that would be nice because it is so hot here. Mr. Li said it is good for crops, however. Already in the south one rice crop has been harvested, and in about a month another one will be. Wheat and grains are excellent this year, but the Chinese are worried about next year because streams and reservoirs are low.

The subject of age often comes up with the Chinese. They revere old age; many of their leaders are over seventy; and yet individuals seem sensitive about their own age. I remember Madame Soong being terribly upset when in one of his articles Harrison said that she was older than she was. It was the fault of the *New York Times*, their record was wrong, but H. got the blame.

Mr. Li complained that the foreign press says he is older than he is, which, he said, is sixty-seven. That makes him a year younger than Harrison, and he remarked that no matter how he tried to make a "Great Leap Forward," he couldn't get ahead of H. He seemed pleased that he is younger, but some people have suggested to us that he is really not.

We thanked him for the opportunity of talking with him, and whirled back to the hotel.

Tomorrow morning we go to the airport to watch Tito arrive, then lunch with Saul Adler, and to Taching at 7:40 P.M. on the train.

Wednesday, August 31,
on the train to Taching

YESTERDAY MORNING we went out to the airport (fourth time in a week) and watched Tito arrive for a state visit. Five thousand people were assembled in Tien An-Men Square, mostly children and young people in brightly colored clothes waving streamers and huge pom-poms and flowers. They had been lined up since early morning. Five thousand more were out at the Guest House, on the outskirts of Peking, where Tito is staying.

On our previous visit we watched the arrival of Madame Bandanarike from Sri Lanka, and it seemed to me there was more red carpet than today, but Mr. Mao said no. There is, and was, he said, red carpet only on the steps up to the door of the plane.

All the diplomats were on hand except for the Americans from the Liaison Office because, while we have this office here, we are not on official diplomatic terms with China. The diplomats were an impressive sight—many Africans in their marvelous bright-colored robes and turbans—lined up in front of the terminal building. Soldiers, more children, and young people waving flags and banners added up to several hundred more welcomers. We (the press) stood on a three-tiered platform like an auctioning block, so I could see well.

Chairman Hua, all the vice-chairmen, Foreign Minister Huang Hua, Madame Ho, and others—all the important people in the government—were on hand to greet Tito.

For any age, and he is eighty-six, Tito looks terrific. He is a big man, tan and fit. He walked around the airfield accompanied by all the Chinese, in the broiling sun, reviewed the soldiers and young dancers and greeters, then came down the line of ambassadors and shook hands with every one of them. He was immaculately and smartly dressed, and his hair must be dyed, because it is a soft brown and nicely waved on top. H. says he has always cared about his looks and is quite a ladies' man.

We were caught up in the parade of cars and had to follow them around the big square in Peking, so were half an hour late to lunch with the Adlers. We met them at the Hsin Chiao Hotel, where the Coes had taken us for dinner. The Adlers have lived there for a year now because their house was damaged in the earthquake last year. They have a bedroom and a big living room, but most of their things are in storage, and they especially miss their books. They still don't know if the Chinese will rebuild their house, which was an old one, or will tear down what's left and put up an apartment house.

Of Russian-Jewish background, Saul Adler was born and brought up in London. He attended the London School of Economics and came to the United States some time before the New Deal. He went to work as an economist for the Treasury Department and at the time of World War II was sent to Chungking as Treasury Department head there. He came back to Washington in 1945 or 1946 and was still working for the Treasury at the time of the great communist witch-hunt in the 1950s.

He was accused of being a communist, investigated along with Frank Coe and others, among them Harry Dexter White, a high official in the department who subsequently died of a heart attack. Adler decided to come back to China and has lived here ever since.

He is the picture of an English eccentric—tall but bent over a bit the way very thin, hollow-chested people sometimes stand; long hair cut straight across the ends; baggy pants. He talks and gesticulates constantly, and I thought he was terribly nice and funny. Mrs. Adler is English and must be quite a lot younger. We had a delicious Chinese lunch in the hotel dining room and went up to their living room for melon and coffee.

I am interested that foreigners who have lived here for twenty years or more cannot read or converse in Chinese. Mr. Adler speaks a little, but Mrs. Adler does not, even though she teaches English in the foreign-language school.

The conversation went so fast from subject to subject that I couldn't really keep track of anything.

After lunch we went shopping and bought an overnight suitcase called The Long March, for me. Even knowing what I do about traveling, I forgot to bring a small bag, which is essential for a trip like this in which we go off to places for a few days but return to Peking.

This is a comfortable, clean train, and we are being treated royally. We have a four-bed compartment to ourselves. On the table between the beds is a blue glass lamp with a red and white shade and a cactus plant growing in a flowerpot. A plastic cover keeps the other two covers on the table clean. Plastic covers the tables in the dining car also and flowerpots with different kinds of flowers are on each.

As is customary, we had breakfast entirely alone in the dining car. I had forgotten about the warm, sweet milk they give us when we ask for milk with coffee. It is like childhood suppers. At lunch Mr. Mao sat with us, and Chinese were eating at other tables. It was nice and natural.

We had a good night's rest, went to sleep at nine and awoke at seven-thirty. The roadbeds are smooth, and trains don't go very fast in China, so it was not bumpy. I got up once and went to the toilet, which is at the end of the car, and this morning Mr. Mao said he was afraid I hadn't slept well, had been awake. No secrets in this country!!

Later—at Taching

TACHING MEANS "great celebration." It represents the celebration of finding oil at the time of the Tenth Party Congress.

We got here at four in the afternoon. Twenty years ago

this whole area was just plains, a continuation of the great Manchurian plain. Now it is the biggest oil field in China and one of the biggest in the world. There are many lakes, therefore many puddles for ducks and geese. Also, we see goats here—we saw none on our last trip. The Chinese don't eat cheese, and they don't drink milk the way we do. Mr. Mao told us that they call our old friend Yao Wei a foreigner because he likes cheese and meat. Goats are used for meat here.

We are in a big new guest house with many rooms and courtyards, high ceilings, all brick and cement and stucco—stark contemporary Chinese interiors. There are a few cockroaches and some flies, and we have been told not to open the windows because of the mosquitoes. Maddening—because here is where the air is clean and fresh and cool. It all points to the lessened use of pesticides, which is good, but maybe the bugs are resistant. I wish we had some screens; I am suffocating.

Upon arrival we had the usual briefing about what we want to do and where we are to go, then a bath followed by a dinner given by the head of the reception committee—a typical bureaucrat, I would say. The dining room is through a courtyard and in another building. We sat in a special section marked off by screens, so we couldn't tell who else might be there or how many. Also, there are no trees and no plantings in the courtyards, which are big, so it adds to the starkness.

Thursday, September 1, 7:45 P.M., Taching

BEING HERE, staying in this peculiar place, and what we did today are all reasons why I did *not* want to come back to China. We are in a newly built guest house which is perfectly adequate except for what I wrote last night. The bathroom floor is always wet and disgusting. The bedroom floor is cement and has no rug—hard to do exercises on. There are flies and cockroaches, and we can't open the windows. A whole section of this house already has screens and the rooms are empty, but we're here in this part without screens. That seems more like the Soviet Union than China, because the Chinese are obviously concerned about our welfare and comfort, whereas I never felt the Russians cared at all. I guess the Chinese just don't think about some things. They are so disciplined from birth that I don't believe personal comfort ever occurs to them.

All day we went to tiresome things. First of all, this morning we had a tour of the Taching Exhibition Hall. Room after room shows the development of this area from barren plains to what it is today, in photographs, charts, models, and maps. The life of their great hero, Wang Chiu-hsi, the Iron Man of Taching, is portrayed in pictures and drawings. Several girl guides shouted his story in high-pitched voices. He worked hard even when he was sick; he met Chou En-lai and was praised by him; he jumped into a vat of cement to keep it from hardening. He is an inspiration to every worker. (Recent visitors to China report that this hero was tortured by the Gang of Four and died in prison.) One girl was lovely. She has studied English, speaks with a British accent, looked eighteen, though she is twenty-five.

After a good lunch we drove for half an hour to a drilling-team headquarters and saw what that group of eighty-five people do. Nothing that is necessary, Harrison said. The drilling has all been done, everything is automatic, one person could do what they do. But politically it is important. They have a clinic and a library and have a lot of meetings and discussions of Marx, Lenin, and Maoism.

It interests me that wages have not changed since 1971, though in an article Fox Butterfield says that they haven't changed since the 1950s. I would think it would be discouraging year after year never to get more pay. If and when there is an increase, it will be countrywide, the same in every factory and commune. (Recently an increase in wages has been reported.)

We are to stay here tomorrow night, too, and go to Harbin on the train Saturday. I hope we go back to Peking on Sunday as planned, but who knows? Plans change for no apparant reason.

Friday, September 2, 1 P.M.

LAST NIGHT we had supper at 6:00 P.M., and I went to bed and to sleep at 8:30. Except for waking up occasionally from flies, I slept until 5:45 A.M.—nearly ten hours. That must illustrate how tiring this country is.

This morning we jounced over bumpy roads in the Chinese Volkswagen bus we travel in here, for about thirty-five minutes to a supply command post of a village. Sometimes I get translations wrong, and I wrote down that it was the Dust Pan area, which seemed very appropriate to me, but Harrison says its the Duck Pen mountain command post. Except for ducks, that makes no sense to me. Nothing is in a pen (horses, donkeys, pigs, chickens, as well as ducks, are loose everywhere), and there are no mountains as far as we can see.

Anyway, the Chinese have a good plan here for building from scratch. There is a central township surrounded by four villages. In other words, like street committees in the cities, society, or whatever you want to call it—people—are divided into groups that are manageable and workable. There are about thirty thousand people living here now, and instead of creating an "oil city," they live in small units. They have a big agricultural project, and it works because the area is divided into several sections, each with housing and fields for crops alongside the oil wells.

I must say it is dreary. Before oil production intensified, it must have been just plains, really like our prairie, which has also vanished. Oil was discovered forty-two years ago, before the Revolution, but nothing much was done until 1960.

There are wells everywhere. Most have just the customary small pumps, but in many cases the pressure is so low they have to use a larger pump to pump water into the well to increase the pressure.

I have never been to an oil field before and was surprised that there is no work to do except watching over a lot of machinery inside buildings and keeping track of gauges and meters.

There are many flowers planted around the buildings —cosmos, zinnias, hollyhocks. I saw a large orange butterfly and a dragonfly. Also there are swallows outside our window, and when we do open it in the daytime, they come very close to flying in. There are sparrows, too, and Mr. Mao says sparrow soup is very good. (That might be a good idea for us to cultivate to cut down the English sparrow population at home, where they are a menace to most songbirds.) I imagine most oil fields don't have flowers and trees, but that is the essence of this society—they have everything together, and it does make sense. Fields of corn and cabbage grow on top of the oil fields; housing is in clusters; people can get out to where they work easily. The township seems like our federal government; it has some control and say-so about the surrounding villages, but the villagers have their own management.

There is no busing here. Children go to nurseries, kindergarten, and then to schools in their own communities.

We visited the local store for the area and bought a calligraphy brush made from the hair of a wolf's tail and a tube of red oil paint for our daughter Ellen. The brush cost about $1.65 and the paint 30¢. I noticed the black sandals that both men and women wear—the best kind cost seven yuan, which is about $3.50, and the sneaker kind cost $3.00 to $4.00. If you make only sixty yuan a month, that's quite a lot to pay for shoes.

Other products were what I'd expect in a general store—towels, material, socks, shirts, wool for knitting, pens, mirrors, thermometers, etc., etc., and a section for food, cookies, bread, canned things, and liquor—all quite expensive. People who live here buy most of the food they don't grow themselves in a different shop that's not for show. We see them lined up outside the door several times a day.

Saturday, September 3, 5 P.M.

I STOPPED TAKING notes at all the stops we made because it is so repetitive. We were going to keep track of how many times we heard "the Gang of Four," but we couldn't possibly. And we were going to keep track of flies, the way we did last time, but that is impossible too.

Harrison says it is obvious the cadres feel superior to the workers—he has seen several instances of it, especially in the girls in managerial positions lording it over the ordinary worker. For instance, the girl who took us around a pig farm in a village ordered the women in the pig pens to get all the pigs out of their houses and into the yard. They blow a whistle, and the pigs come out. She made three or four women do it again and again, and none of them seemed pleased. Imagine having to spend most of the day actually in a pig pen with about fifty pigs, shoveling up their manure as soon as they excrete it and then hurling it over the fence. I am sympathetic to the Chinese attitude about physical labor and agree that everyone should know how to do as much as possible and realize how much work goes into caring for animals and growing food. But I felt it was humiliating to those women to be asked to perform in the pig pen for foreigners, and I imagine that was the purpose.

This morning in the mending and making-over clothes department or factory H. saw the head woman take a piece of material and hurl it at a worker in a very insulting manner. Sounds like human nature, also the Soviet Union, not the China where people are taught to love and care for each other.

At the above factory we saw how they take the most worn-out workers' clothes and remake them into something useful. The filthy clothes are first pulled apart, then the pieces are washed in the most primitive laundry except for a stream that I have ever seen. I said to H., "Is that a washing machine?" and he said yes, they put the clothes in that vessel (it was like an oil drum, which it probably was) and stir them around with a stick. After washing, the pieces were thrown outdoors in heaps, not hung up, to dry. I saw one woman walking into a room with an electric iron in her hand, but I didn't see one in use.

They make new padded jackets and trousers with new cotton filling and new outside material, but the linings are made of the old pieces, sewn together in patchwork. They use all the old stuffing and pieces of material that can't be used in the half-new jackets and trousers to make mattresses. The old stuff is made into sheets of a sort of heavy felt and put in plain heavy cotton covers with buttons to keep the lining from bunching up. It is pretty primitive and didn't appeal to me much, but when compared with the alternative—a pile of straw or nothing —it is quite nice, even luxurious.

Next we visited a workshop that may be the only one of its kind in the world. Here the wires that had been burned out of light bulbs were being removed and new ones inserted. A hole was made in the top of the bulb; with tweezers a girl pulled out the defective wire and put in a new one. Then the glass was heated and melted and sealed up. Repaired builbs are tested with high voltage and when the electricity was connected to the testing apparatus, there were several loud pops as some made-over bulbs burned out again.

It is a good way to keep otherwise idle hands busy and to promote the idea of saving and using everything, but it doesn't seem very efficient or worthwhile as far as light bulbs are concerned.

The conditions up here look awful to me. When I think of the figure exhibits of poor peasants being exploited by wicked landlords and living in earth huts or caves, the present houses don't look much better. It is so dusty and grimy; there are not many trees except around the business buildings; and whole areas of houses stand like toy houses stretching out for miles in a flat, barren, dusty plain. Of course there are settlements of houses—villages, then fields of crops, and another village. But nothing is finished; dirty bricks are heaped around the houses, piles of dirt and sand and sticks, nothing underfoot but packed-down dirt and clay, grayish brown. Chickens roam at will; in many areas there are puddles with ducks and geese; and, as I said before, there are quite a few goats, which they eat. In Peking I asked about the goats we saw on the outskirts of the city, asked if they were for food, and was told no, in a rather shocked voice.

There seem to be lots of children who are not in a nursery or kindergarten, though we did visit a kindergarten with three small sections. Many children are just playing around in the dust near the houses. In the kindergarten we were entertained by the usual dances and recitations. It never ceases to amuse and amaze me to hear tiny tots singing about their hearts belonging to Chairman Mao (not Daddy) and doing a baby's dance warmly celebrating the Eleventh Party Congress. No American who hasn't seen and heard this kind of thing can believe or understand this part of Chinese indoctrination. And even seeing it often, it is still hard to believe.

But the biggest miracle to me is that they don't have terrible epidemics and disease anymore. Harrison says it's because they boil all their water, and members of the Revolutionary Committee see to it that they do, and everyone is inoculated and vaccinated against childhood diseases as well as others that were so prevalent—malaria and cholera, etc. Even so, mosquitoes are the reason we can't open our windows at night here. I killed one in the bathroom, and that is all I have seen, but the flies are awful.

So we have to judge what we see against what we know it once was: Grubby, dusty, and primitive are not the same as ignorant, exploited, starving, and diseased.

We went to a petrochemical plant that was impressive and very up to date. But it doesn't mean much to me. It is fascinating how many products can be made from oil besides the obvious gas, kerosene, and wax. I am always amazed that yarn for knitting and weaving material comes from oil, as well as a substance for fertilizer. Maybe the last is not so queer, because oil is a natural product and does come out of the ground.

Sunday, September 4, on the airplane from Harbin to Peking, 5:30 P.M.

LAST NIGHT at seven we took the train from Taching to Harbin, a three-hour ride in the "soft sleeping" car, though of course we didn't go to bed. Instead of identifying train cars as they really are, in terms of first, second, and third class, they are referred to as "soft sleeping," "hard sleeping," and "hard sitting." Many Chinese were in the same car as we were, as on the train from Peking. I slept most of the time, and H. talked to Mr. Mao. He is such a very nice man and knows a lot about the United States and Russia, but eats up everything H. says, and H. likes to talk.

At Harbin we were met by Mr. Ting, who speaks precise English with an English accent and who was a classmate of Mr. Mao in the university. They haven't seen each other for twenty years. I think that's very strange, because this is really such a familial setup, and everyone seems to know each other, at least in the top echelon, which is all we are ever really exposed to. Harrison asked me how many of my classmates I keep in touch with, but that is very different. I went to boarding school with girls from the Middle West, West, and South, only a few from the East, where I come from. During the war, when I was living all over the country, I ran into several schoolmates but have kept up with only one. We married different kinds of men, have had different kinds of lives, and there have never been reasons to meet. Here in China they all belong to the same club, so to speak, and work for the same company.

The hotel in Harbin was built by the Japanese in 1930 and, I imagine, was very comfortable and classy in those days. Now it has gone the way of all former, not necessarily luxurious, but attractive and neat and clean hotels. The carpets must be the original ones installed by the Japanese. In the halls and on the stairs they are red and worse than shabby; they are worn, torn, generally dirty, and not fastened down securely, so you can easily trip. Our room was all right—two comfortable beds and a clothes cupboard (hardly merits the term *armoire*) with a mirror almost as cockeyed as the mirrors in amusement parks that distort you. But from my bed I could see that no one had dusted or mopped under it for weeks. And the bathroom was revolting, just as it was in Taching.

For some reason they have an open drain in the middle of all bathroom floors, covered only with mesh or grating. I imagine it must connect with all the drains from all the other bathrooms, because often, for no apparant reason, a ghastly smell permeates the place. If the drains were flushed and cleaned and if they scrubbed the floors, it wouldn't be so unattractive. In the Harbin bathroom the tiles had been crudely cut and left jagged.

In Taching some pipe leaked, and the floor was not cleaned the whole time we were there. I left two pieces of paper on the floor just to see, and they stayed in the same place for three days.

If I were the Chinese, I would teach the hundreds of people they have working in the hotels really how to clean. They spend a lot of time getting up on ladders and tables and chairs to wipe off lights and high windows, but I would like to show them how to properly clean a bathroom, top to bottom, and make it shine. Maybe it's part of the great proletarian society not to put emphasis on appearance or aesthetics, but cleanliness is one of their great maxims, and I think they could do better without sacrificing any revolutionary or socialist spirit. (They shouldn't use that word *socialism* the way they do; what they have is not socialism, it's dictatorship from the top, not of the proletariat. The top may be made up from the proletariat group, but the individual proletariat has no voice in the government.)

The bottom sheets on our beds had very nice embroidery on one end, but we had the Russian kind of blanket inside a cover, so there was no need for the usual top sheet. The embroidery hung over the foot of each bed, and I wouldn't have noticed it except that I took the spread off in order to lie on the floor to do some exercises. It was a relief to be able to open the window, and the air in Harbin was nice—much cooler than in Peking, and no bugs.

This morning we had breakfast at seven-thirty, and at eight-thirty went for a combination sight-seeing drive and visit to a heavy-generator factory. The latter was not interesting to me except for a good and honest talk about the Gang of Four, from a member of the Revolutionary Committee, and a wonderful set of posters about the Gang in the factory. H. took some pictures, but he only has black and white film. I should have taken some, but usually indoor pictures don't come out for me. One poster showed a tree that represented Lin Piao with four crows sitting on it; one was of Chiang Ching, another was Wang asleep, dreaming of power. He is the youngest of the Gang. One showed Liu Shao-chi and Chiang Ching fighting for power; they were all funny and well drawn.

In the middle of this great, huge factory that manufactures enormous pieces of machinery was a little horse pulling a wagon on which men were piling pieces of wood—maybe from crates? An amazing sight, yet not too surprising in China, where everything is mixed up.

Harbin is quite a nice city, or rather it could be and must once have been. Some buildings are painted pink, some yellow, and in some areas the streets converge on a circle like Washington, D.C. There are flowers and shrubs, lots of lilacs covered with dust. Huge piles of sand for cement are everywhere, spoiling every street. They are for building air raid shelters, which I thought had been completed all over China. Here they feel the Soviet threat more keenly than in the middle of this enormous country.

We were given an excellent lunch by the vice-chairman of the Foreign Office of the province, a very nice woman. Some of the food was reminiscent of Russia—prawns rolled in crumbs and fried like chicken Kiev and served with tiny strips of potato and canned peas. And shaslik, or shish kebab, and red caviar—all very Russian.

Monday, September 5,
Min Zu Hotel, Peking, 4:30 P.M.

MR. LIU, of the Press Department, met us at the plane. I thought it was just a nice, friendly gesture, but H. thinks there was some reason we'll never know behind it. He came with us in our car, and Mr. Mao went in the Ministry car. He asked about our trip and seemed to be trying to find out if we had had a satisfactory visit or if something was wrong. He suggested to H. that he write out in detail what he wanted to do when we go to Shanghai and Hangchow and give it to Mr. Ma, his superior at the Press Department. Then all of a sudden the car in front stopped; we pulled ahead of it and stopped; Mr. Liu got out without even saying good-bye, and Mr. Mao joined us. I rolled down my window and called good-bye to Mr. Liu but he didn't hear. The car whisked away, and Mr. Mao said he was going to the Ministry. Mysterious doings in the middle of the night.

Mr. Liu is the man who chewed out Fox Butterfield for three hours the night he arrived from Hong Kong. He is a sharp little guy and can be very charming, but he has his tough side, too.

84

We asked for a room in the back of this hotel, and it is much nicer and quieter. There is noise, but it is different, and no horns and traffic. Just some machine that they hook up, or goes on, spasmodically, even at night, and today when I was napping there was a lot of hammering.

We went shopping in Chinese stores today and bought bicycle bells, embroidered pillowcases, chopsticks, two cups with covers for H. and me to have our tea in, some thermometers with pictures. I bought some silk scarves in the hotel. They are quite pretty, all silk and cost about $1.50. I'll get some more, for they are really the best presents to take home.

Then lunch and sitting around on our beds. I have a pain in my left side, and I suppose it's rich food. I don't see how people get thin here—everything is drenched with oil, and though I don't really eat much, it's heavy.

We are to dine with Madame Soong tonight and leave at 6 A.M. tomorrow for Inner Mongolia.

9 P.M.

WE ARE BACK from dinner with that fabulous lady. Rewi Alley was there, and Dr. Hatem with his beautiful Chinese wife. He is American and has been here in China and mixed up with the revolutionary people since about 1930. He knew Ed Snow. The lovely older Chinese lady who was with Madame Soong in 1972 was also present, and a young girl whom Madame Soong introduced as "my little girl." She is her ward. She is pretty and sharp and seemed very status-conscious. She was superior and abrupt to the man who led us out and didn't turn on the light as she wished.

It was awfully hot, and as we moved to the dining table, Madame Soong said, "The men can be liberated from their coats." Dinner was delicious. Soup came first, not usual in China, then fried prawns, followed by Peking duck with all the trimmings. Especially good were some light, airy sort of popovers to fill with strips of duck. Next came fish, which I didn't eat—a pretty dish with slices of pineapple and tomato around the edge of the platter; sea slugs, which they politely call sea cucumbers, in the three-delicacy concoction; and a chicken and pepper dish. The meal ended with fruit and almond tea, which is milky and sweet. Much too much. I ate as little as possible and still have the pain in my side. Hope I can manage tomorrow. This is the worst part of traveling—not feeling 100 percent all right. But I think in Mongolia I may not want to do everything that is scheduled, so maybe I can take it easy.

We talked about Chiang Ching and the Gang of Four and Roxanne Witke's book, *Comrade Chiang Ching*. Everyone agreed that Miss Witke was terribly naïve and that Chiang Ching is a megalomaniac and crazy. Whatever Miss Witke's idea was, the book has done her subject nothing but harm.

Chiang Ching and her gang are blamed for all the persecution of intellectuals. The Gang consisted of Chiang Ching, Mao's wife; Chang Chun-chiao, the boss of Shanghai; Yao Wen-yuan, of the Shanghai newspaper

Wen Wei Pao; and Wang Hung-wen, of the Textile Workers' Union, the youngest of the Four, who entertained at fancy dinners, had many "younger brothers" (a Chinese term for a close follower or friend) who did his bidding, and had four automobiles.

In 1965 Chairman Mao and his wife, Chiang Ching, were living most of the time in Shanghai, where she had started her acting career in the 1930s. The active direction of the government had been taken over by Liu Shao-chi; Mao was on the shelf. He decided to attack his opponents and try to regain control.

The mayor of Peking had written a play which was a veiled attack on Mao. Through Chiang Ching, Mao got Yao Wen-yuan, who was literary critic of the newspaper, to write an article criticizing the play. It is such a Chinese roundabout way of doing things—never the direct onslaught.

The article was published in November 1965 in the Shanghai paper and turned out to be the opening shot in what was to become the Cultural Revolution. It is clear now that this turmoil was started by and used by Chairman Mao, his wife, Mr. Yao, Mr. Chang, and Mr. Wang to try to seize power and put Mao back at the head of the government. They are blamed for starting the Cultural Revolution; for letting, and even helping it get out of hand; for the ghastly treatment of Anthony Grey, the English correspondent who was locked up in his house by the Red Guards and not permitted to read any of his own books unless he could remember the title, author, publisher, and date of publication of the volume he asked for; and for all the other horrors, too numerous to write.

According to stories about Chiang Ching, she had several wigs ordered from Paris, all different styles of hairdos. Also, she had 140 dresses made especially for her. Where or when, I wonder, did she wear them?

Madame Soong gave me a pretty embroidered scarf and some flowers, and we left at 8:15 P.M., having arrived there at 6:30. She is more feeble physically than in 1972 and has to be helped up from a chair and to walk. Before dinner we sat in a circle in a corner of the dining room, so no walking was necessary. She is mentally as sharp and amusing as ever, and she is certainly happy with the present government.

Talking to Madame Soong and hearing her ideas makes the whole Gang affair add up more sensibly. It was a continuation of the Cultural Revolution. She said to us, "You must notice how much better the spirit is and how much happier the people are." Well, of course we can't tell about the first, and in Harbin we noticed people not doing their jobs. For example, when we were leaving the factory in Harbin, our guide had to get out of the car and open the gate, in spite of the fact many workers whose job it obviously was were standing around. And there was certainly not much discipline inside the factory. In Peking people seem more independent than I remember; they don't obey traffic rules, and the police are always yelling at them.

But the people we know are far more confident and do seem happier—relieved. We are told that the intellectuals are reappearing, though we haven't seen any yet. Mr. Mao told us about an opera singer who had been sent away to someplace in the country and hadn't been heard from for several years. After the smashing of the Gang she reappeared in Peking and sang a song that no one had been allowed to sing for ten years. The audience wept, he said. It would be like sending Beverly Sills down to a pig farm to mind the pigs. Imagine how everyone would feel at her first reappearance. Of course, it is something I can't imagine.

Painters are painting again, writers are writing stories, not propoganda, so we are told. Shakespeare is going to be published, also Tolstoy, and Beethoven is no longer considered reactionary.

Harrison said to Madame Soong that when we had been here before, she had complained about the food and that no one in China knew how to cook anymore, that the best Chinese restaurant was in Paris. She replied, "They're paying more attention to such things now."

The people we met the last time and those we know are all intellectuals and students. Some of them have been to other countries; most speak English or other languages. Many of them just went down to May Seventh schools and stayed there until the trouble blew over and the Gang was smashed. The young man who in 1972 was chosen to explain the Cultural Revolution to us in Shanghai is out of office (he was one of Wang's "younger brothers"), so is the editor of the newspaper there. Whether they are in camps or still at work being "criticized" and "educated" I don't know.

Tuesday, September 6,
Silinhot, Inner Mongolia, 6 P.M.

WE LEFT PEKING at 7:45, left the hotel at 6:00, and had breakfast at the airport, at least H. and Mr. Mao did. I felt awful and had a terrible headache. Really horrible to feel like this. Anyway, we flew one and a half hours to Huhehot, the capital of Inner Mongolia, and as we got off the plane, I said to H., "I've made it so far, now I'll go to bed here and recover." But no such luck. We were to wait for an hour in the airport, then go to where we are now, miles from any place, in the middle of a desert plain, 125 miles from the Outer Mongolian border, 700 miles from Peking.

As we say to each other nearly every day, and I must have written a hundred times, we have to come to communist countries to be treated as if we were royalty. At the airport we waited in a special waiting room with lots of comfortable chairs and sofas and its own washrooms.

The ladies' toilet was the Asian type, which is oblong and usually level with the floor, or slightly higher. In hotels and many public places they are made of porcelain, and they flush. You do not sit, you squat, and it is sometimes hard on Western legs. But it was clean and private, and it worked. There was a clean towel, fresh soap, and a little jar of cold cream. H. said the men's room had a regular Western toilet—funny.

We finally got here at about 11:30 A.M. It is just a settlement in the plains. H. was told first that the population is 100,000, next time that it is 50,000. We aren't really sure where we are. The map in the Nagel guide doesn't show Silinhot.

We are in one of those big buildings the Chinese have everywhere for guest houses. This one was teeming with people, all Mongolian, when we arrived. We are on the second floor in a suite that has a living room, bedroom, and bath, and what's best, a double bed. The bed isn't made up the way we make them. Over the mattress, which is hard, is a checked cover that looks like a tablecloth. Instead of a blanket is a large piece of toweling, like a striped beach towel and a silk comforter inside a washable cover. The pillows have pretty embroidered cases.

Both rooms have been freshly painted with white walls and baby blue enamel paint up to about as high as my chest. A pair of pajamas for each of us, embroidered ones for me, and two terry cloth bathrobes are in the cupboard. The United States editors and publishers who were just in Mongolia, but not up here, complained that the tubs were so filthy they couldn't take baths, but ours is spotless. It is quite long and sits on a concrete base about one foot high. H. says they got the idea from the Ming Tombs.

I have been in bed since we arrived and am going to stay here. I have slept a lot and drunk gallons of very weak tea and hot water. Poor Harrison went down to lunch and found there was a table for us and right next to it, but behind a screen, a table for Mr. Mao and our host here, who is a tall, big Chinese man and a leading member of the Revolutionary Committee, and also the man from the Provincial Foreign Office of Mongolia, who met us at Huhehot and accompanied us here.

It is strange, this custom of isolating everyone while they eat, as if we were diseased. And I always feel that no Chinese man wants to sit next to me. When we have to ride three in the back seat of the car, they always seem happier if Harrison is in the middle. I don't think this is my imagination. Mr. Mao says they separate us at meals out of consideration, that people have different customs and ways of eating and are probably happier and more at ease eating alone or with their countrymen. And that it is hard to be an interpreter all the time and then have to continue interpreting while eating. So I guess there is some point after all, except that Chinese-speaking visitors, and even overseas Chinese (Chinese who are born abroad) are treated the same way. But Mr. Mao was polite and ate with H. on the wrong side of the screen for him.

This makes me think of a woman I know who has just been in Peking. In her hotel dining room one day she noticed a handsome black man sitting by himself. He looked lonely, so she went over to him and said, "I am an American, and I wonder if you are too." He replied, no, that he came from Tanzania. She said she knew his country, had been there several times, and they talked for a while. He was a doctor, highly educated, who had been studying in Germany before coming to China and was now studying Chinese medicine and surgery. He told my friend that she was the first person who had spoken to him in the several months he had been in this country. The Chinese he studied with were polite and pleasant in the classrooms and the hospital, but no one had spoken to him outside that milieu. No one had asked him to have lunch or dinner, either in his or her home or in a restaurant. No one had asked him to go for a walk, visit a museum, see a movie, or shown any interest in how he was getting along outside the classes. And he was lonely.

While Harrison was having his lunch and I was in bed asleep, someone came and left a bowl of eight warm freshly boiled eggs and some cake in our sitting room—a touching, caring gesture.

H. went to a paper factory this afternoon where paper is made from willows and shrubs that have been planted here. He said several Chinese girls were folding the paper, and he thinks they are city girls who were first sent to the pig farms and now have been elevated to factory jobs.

He saw the only lama temple here in the town and says it is a mess. The walls are hacked down, rooms and windows added, many people live in it. There are other temples around, but they are being allowed to disintegrate and collapse. I suppose we can't blame the people for not wanting to preserve the temples and monasteries and landlords' houses. The system was terribly repressive. They must hate to see reminders of it. Rewi Alley told me that when he first came to Inner Mongolia with Ed Snow in the 1920s, they helped bury 140,000 people who had died of famine. That was usual and scarcely noticed by the ruling class. Obviously the old way had to be thrown over. Dr. Hatem, who was at Madame Soong's for dinner the other night (heavens, it was only last night) was instrumental in wiping out venereal disease here. I don't mean this actual town, but all of Inner Mongolia, which has been populated by Chinese farmers, peasants, and landlords for many years. There are more Chinese than Mongols in Inner Mongolia today.

Our "suite" is at the back of this building, and from our second-floor windows we look out on a big pile of coal dust and to the right of that a small building which must be for supplies because the door is kept locked. (Incidently, many closets and cupboards and desk drawers were locked in Taching—a great change from our last visit, when everything seemed to be out in the open.) I saw one man unlock the door and emerge with a basket of eggplant. He left a large gunnysack, probably of potatoes, on the ground, locked the door, and pocketed the key. Whereupon three children, one just a toddler, the others girls of about six or seven, appeared with one of those wonderful homemade baby carriages and tried for a while to move the sack. They couldn't budge it, naturally, but their father soon appeared, lifted it into the baby carriage, picked up the baby, and off they went.

All afternoon, trucks loaded with coal dust have driven

up. Usually two, sometimes three, girls would shovel off the black stuff onto the pile. They wore no gloves, but their hair was covered with the same gauzy material the Outer Mongolian women use, and tied in the same way. Once the driver, a man, squatted on the ground and smoked a cigarette while the girls shoveled. The air is heavenly here, but I shut the window each time a truck came.

Beyond the coal pile is a row of several attached one-story houses in the usual Chinese plan, with a door in between two windows—Chinese townhouses of two or three rooms each. Children have been playing, two men sat on stools weaving baskets, another was washing his clothes in a basin. Women, I couldn't tell if they were mothers or grandmothers, appeared occasionally in the doorways to check on the children. Three pigs wandered here and there, through the coal pile, which turned them black, and in and out of the houses.

On the plane from Peking this morning Mr. Mao sat next to a Mongol dancer, Modegema, who was famous before the Cultural Revolution but had not been permitted to dance for eight years. She is small and pretty and only thirty-seven years old now. Chou En-lai had seen her dance when she was fifteen and was helpful in getting her into the National Song and Dance Assembly. During the Cultural Revolution she was "criticized," and she in turn criticized Chiang Ching and the Gang. She was ordered to stop dancing and was sent to a pig farm. She put up a picture of Premier Chou, was asked why she didn't put up one of Mao. She replied that she didn't have

one of Mao, and what was wrong with a picture of Chou?
She was threatened, was afraid she would be sent to a
"certain place"—prison—for many years. When she
heard of the smashing of the Gang, she sang and danced
for three days, she told Mr. Mao.

Later, just before going to bed for the night

HARRISON WENT down to dinner alone and ate with our
hosts. He said he has never seen such drinking—we are
the excuse for banquets, and it got very rowdy. Thank
God I wasn't there. I stayed up here and got as far as the
sofa in the living room. About half an hour after H. went
down two girls knocked at the door and came in bearing a
tray with a tureen of soup. The soup was oxtail with
noodles and three poached eggs floating on top. As I had
already eaten two boiled eggs, I just had the soup, and it
was very good. Our hosts told H. that an Englishman had
been here (it must have been Neville Maxwell) and was
most pleased to have oxtail soup because since it is now so
expensive in London, he hardly ever eats it.

The girls were awfully sweet and kept looking at me as
if I were the queerest thing they have ever seen, and I
guess I am. A big—compared to them—white woman
who feels sick—ugh!

Wednesday, September 7, 8:30 P.M.

SOMEHOW I survived. The day of sleeping and drinking tea was what I needed. The headache has gone and I don't feel sick and shaky any more. But I am terribly homesick, something I have never been and never understood. The other day at the factory in Harbin when Harrison was listening to all the usual details about production and Mao and the Gang of Four, I became so homesick I thought I would cry right there. Tears came into my eyes, and I had to make a big effort to act normal. Tonight I didn't make that effort. When we got back from a really exhausting day, there was no hot water, and the toilet tank, which is high up on the wall and has a chain, like those in my grandmother's house, dripped constantly so the floor was sopping wet, and water splashed on my back when I sat on the toilet. I washed in the cold water, put on my wrapper, lay down on the strange bed, and burst into tears. At my age. It is hard to believe. We are so terribly far away. I miss the children and grandchildren. I think about our house all alone, my garden suffocating in weeds, the new pond we just built and can't watch fill up. I was sick at home before we started out, and I guess I never really recovered and have been "below par," as my mother used to say, all along.

Well, I got over it. We had supper (I didn't eat much), and now H. has gone to a movie that is going to last two hours, which I didn't feel up to. Last night he saw some interesting documentaries. One was about sheep dying from a poisonous plant that grows on some of the prairies; immediately after eating it the sheep shake all over and die in minutes. The film showed people rushing out and digging up by hand every poisonous plant for hundreds of miles around.

Another explained their tree-planting program, which is remarkable. Trees don't grow here normally; the wind is so strong they can't stand it, and the soil is hard clay, only about three feet deep, so the roots can't go down. I should think they'd try pine trees, which spread their roots out, not down. I noticed that some trees planted outside the hospital of the commune were tied to a rail fence to keep them from blowing over. They build remarkable walls about five feet high of soil and grass to surround the tree nurseries and vegetable plots to protect them from the wind.

This morning at seven we had breakfast—boiled eggs and coffee with hot milk. A dish of cookies was on the table, but we didn't eat any. At eight we set out to visit a commune devoted to livestock, in a car with Mr. Mao sitting with Harrison and me in the back and our local host, the big Chinese man, in front with the driver. The pretty girl who is on the staff of the Information Office of Mongolia rode ahead of us in a jeep. Her name means "flower in bloom" in Mongol. She seems like a fervent party member. Another car with the man from Huhehot and some others followed behind.

We drove for about forty-five minutes over terrain just like Outer Mongolia—no roads, just jeep tracks—flat, dusty plains. Here and there were groups of sheep, horses, and cattle. I saw only one yurt (tent) until we visited one. Usually the herdsmen live in brick houses in the winter and move about the plains living in yurts in summer. They have camels, but I didn't see any.

A little distance from the commune a jeep was stopped, and two of our local hosts were standing with some other men, obviously waiting for us. They wore bright blue *dals* (Mongolian national dress) and yellow sashes, just like the one I have at home that I got in Ulan Bator, only theirs had gold trimming and mine is silver. The two men looked awkward and uncomfortable, and their dals were brand-new.

We got out, shook hands as if we had never seen those two men before, got back in the car, and drove to the commune headquarters. We were ushered into a one-story brick building that made up one side of a large courtyard, with similar buildings on three sides and the typical outdoor toilet shed at the far end. Down a whitewashed stone corridor, past square rooms with beds or just a table, or desk and chairs, to a room twice the size of those we had passed. In this room was a groaning board if I have ever seen one. Big enough for eight chairs on each side and two at the ends, it was covered with a pretty embroidered cloth, on top of which was another of blue plastic. The table was loaded with every kind of Mongolian specialty you can think of. Several kinds of cheese; several forms of butter; sour cream; a sort of yogurt; cream, cakes, cookies; things that looked like pretzels. Bowls of millet and the tea I can't stand the taste of which I first encountered in Sikkim in 1966. Butter tea, they called it there, or five-element tea. Here it is Mongolian tea. It consists of tea, water, salt, butter, and some sort of thickening, and always tastes rancid or stale to me. Often it is so thick you have to eat it with a spoon, but here it is liquid.

It was only a short time since breakfast, but everything was urged upon us. I discovered that millet seeds are good to nibble, and I asked for regular tea, so got through the first session at the table comfortably.

We sat down—thank heaven the custom is for me to sit next to Harrison with Mr. Mao on my other side—and were briefed with the usual statistics and comments about how they couldn't have done what they have without Chairman Mao's advice and thoughts.

This is the Ta Pu Hsi-la Commune, which means "Great Leap Forward" in Mongel, and was started in 1958 at the time of the Great Leap. Before Liberation the population was 400, with 130 households. Most herdsmen were slaves of the aristocracy and also suffered from foreign invaders. At present, out of 1,702 population, 1,149 are Mongels and only 510 are Han Chinese, plus a handful of other minorities.

Harrison asked what was the reason for the big increase in population, and they answered it was "by natural increase mostly, but also from improved health." They say there is no persuading or teaching family planning to minorities unless they want it. Mongels can marry at age eighteen for girls and twenty for boys, and they often have as many as five or seven children. Syphilis used to be a terrible manace here and all through Inner Mongolia. Dr. Hatem, whom we met at Madame Soong's, was involved with medical teams that were sent from Peking, and they say that venereal disease was wiped out in 1953-54.

The Ta Pu Hsi-la Commune is a livestock commune, and they have only animals. I didn't see anything growing, not a vegetable or a flower. By tradition the Mongols' diet consists of meat, milk, and milk products. They are nomadic people who, before the influence of the Chinese here and the Russians in Outer Mongolia, were made up of tribes living in tents while their animals grazed on the tall grasses of this huge tableland of Central Asia that Harrison calls "back of beyond." They had no agriculture, grew no food; they folded their tents and moved on when the high grasses were eaten over. The vegetables they eat now come from nearby agricultural communes. They burn dung for fuel—there are high piles of it near every house. There is no wood. There are two coal mines in the area, but it is expensive to haul the coal.

They said that 50 percent of the herdsmen have settled down in houses. The others still take the herds from place to place on the plains and live in tents. The settled people are trying to grow good-quality hay, to plant trees for forestation, to make animal sheds. They surround the pastures and agricultural plots with those remarkable mud walls. We were told that the herdsmen have built socialism with their own hands and that they study Mao and the other four heros—Marx, Engels, Lenin, and Stalin. I wonder.

They said that before Liberation, people didn't speak Mongol. Now every brigade has its own schools and teaches in its own language. That's not very convincing either. There are 393 schoolchildren of primary-school age, and 352 are in school. Some Mongol parents still want to keep their children at home, and the Chinese do not force them to attend. Cadres try to persuade the parents of the value of educating their children. It is really a matter of educating the parents. The point of the education is to learn the proletarian point of view, intellectually, politically, and physically. In school the Mongols generally study in Mongol, while the Hans study in Han.

We asked the questions we always ask: Do the cows have brucellosis (or what I have always known as Bangs disease)? And if so, what do they do about it? The answer was no, and there was no real answer about prevention. They only vaccinate against hoof-and-mouth disease. They have a veterinary office, so they must have some program of inoculation and inspection the way we have.

We made the rounds—to two classrooms where Mongol teachers were teaching in Mongol, one counting to music—elementary arithmetic, I guess you'd call it—and another an algebra course. The teacher was demonstrating on the blackboard, and it was very clear. The children seemed young to be learning algebra, about nine or ten, but maybe I've forgotten when I studied it. Both teachers wore the traditional Mongolian *dal*.

Our host in the commune was a Mongol who spoke Mongol to another Mongol who translated into Chinese for Mr. Mao, and he translated into English for us. Obviously certain things get confused, are lost, and we miss a lot, but we always ask when we don't understand and go to great lengths to get things straight.

At the hospital we met doctors of Mongolian and Western medicine and saw all the facilities. The Mongol doctor was a shiny, rosy-faced young man with a perpetual smile, the most cheery doctor I've ever seen. He was examining a young Mongol woman who looked about sixteen but was twenty-seven and had two children. She was suffering from weakness, and she did look awfully tired. The doctor took her pulse on her right wrist, then on the left—a practice we thought strange until it was explained to us that this is the usual routine, to determine the heartbeat on one wrist and the strength on the other. The diagnosis was "weakness," and medicine was prescribed. The doctor took several little triangles of folded paper out of different jars, put them in an envelope, and told her when and how many to take. I couldn't see if they contained pills or powders.

In the Western medicine office a man who hadn't slept

for three nights was having his blood pressure taken. He was given some pills to build him up and was told to return in a few days.

The operating room was simple and clean and had lights over the operating table. We were told they do stomach operations, sterilizations, appendixes, and abortions. Whenever I ask in a hospital what operations are performed, they always mention abortions, yet at clinics and other meetings they say there is no need for abortions because birth control is so widely practiced. Maybe people are persuaded to use it, but if they don't allow themselves to be persuaded, they are in trouble. I asked what kind of contraceptive they suggest, and at the birth control clinic in the hospital the attendant showed us a glass jar with metal rings of different sizes in disinfectant. It is a form of IUD, and I seem to remember back in the 1930s when a friend of mine had a gold ring put in. It was supposed to be quite advanced, but it caused infection and was removed.

Out here we see what the head of the Institute for Minorities in Peking told us—that a few representatives from minority areas are sent to Peking to learn the Chinese language and the theories of Maoism and socialist thought. (They keep referring to their "socialist state." But that is what Sweden has, and in two visits to China I have found little resemblance between the two systems.) Then they return to their villages to help their own people to live by and understand Mao's thoughts. Cadres from Peking are sent here and encouraged to learn the minority language. Obviously they can be much more helpful if they do. Mongol cadres in the commune rarely speak Chinese.

After these visits we returned to the groaning board for the most peculiar lunch Ive ever attended. But first I had to go to the toilet. I tried to put it off but just couldn't get through the whole day. And what a production it can be.

First of all, in a place like this, I have to tell Mr. Mao my problem. I could no more just go to where I see a toilet than I could swim the Pacific—all of Mongolia would be in an uproar. So I begin as if I were telling my nurse I need to go to the bathroom. In earshot of everyone, Mr. Mao told a girl from the commune, who led me across the yard—the toilet was about five hundred feet away at the end of the complex of houses. Halfway we were met by the pretty Mongol girl who rides in the jeep, who had just emerged from the toilet herself. She took me over and escorted me back.

Outdoor Chinese toilets are generally two groups of holes on a platform over a trench surrounded by a brick wall with a partition in the middle separating the men's and women's sides. The characters for male and female are painted large and clear on the front. The entrances are at the back on each side. You are not visible from the outside, but there is no privacy inside unless you're alone, and you can't count on that. Discreetly my escort waited for me outside.

I have been to plenty of outhouses, privies, and toilets in my own country and all over the world, and to similar toilets in other Chinese communes, and this was pretty bad. Two oblong holes with a flimsy piece of wood about two feet high between them opened into the trench. There were a few traces of lime on the ground outside, but none inside, and none in the trench. It hadn't been cleaned out for a long time. I survived, but just, and when I came out, I must have looked rather stunned, for the Mongol girl put her arm around my waist, and thus we walked back across the long yard to the men, who were waiting for me.

We sat down again at that heavily laden table, and in addition to all the things already on it, platter after platter was brought in. Huge plates of mutton, boiled on the bones with all the fat, the most favored part to Mongols. Then countless other dishes: meat and mushrooms, meat and peppers, sliced green and red tomatoes with sugar on top, meat balls, several fried things. Finally rice and very good soup. Our hosts drank a great deal of *mao tai.* "*Gambey,*" ("bottoms up"), they said each time, and most of them did drink bottoms-up all through lunch. They were amused at us—H. doesn't even taste it, and I just wet my tongue. How they can pour even that tiny glassful down their throats is beyond me. It is at least 130 proof (some say 160), and awful tasting.

It was pretty unattractive. They were belching and chewing with their mouths open, smacking their food and spilling *mao tai* all over, making toast after toast. I have been exposed to some hard drinkers in my life, but I have never seen people drink like this. Last night at supper with H. they did the same thing, only worse. Mr. Mao said that if I hadn't been at lunch, they would have drunk much more.

I ate nothing and drank only hot water, which I asked for.

After a brief rest in one of the rooms with beds, we visited a herdsman and his family in their yurt. A yurt, or *ger*, as it is called in Outer Mongolia, is a tent which while portable, seems pretty permanent when you are inside. Mongols have always lived in them while their animals grazed, moving on over the prairie when the grass was eaten. A wooden lattice framework about five and a half or six feet high slopes to form a roof and sides. A hole is left at the top for smoke to escape, and the lattice is covered with felts that are anchored by ropes thrown over and around and attached to stakes in the ground. Since it was a hot summer day, about six inches of lattice near the bottom were not covered and, the dry desert air circulated in and out—Mongolian air-conditioning, and very pleasant. Without that arrangement it would have been stifling.

An opening for the doorway is low (you always have to stoop) and has felt hung overlapping. But today it was pulled aside and fastened to make it cooler. This yurt, which was about twelve to fifteen feet across, as well as the others in this group are smaller than those in Outer Mongolia. The latter are nearer twenty or twenty-five feet across, and the yurt of the abbot at the monastery in Ulan Bator was bigger than that.

A low table stood in the middle of the floor, heaped high with food, and around the edges of the tent were several plain wooden chests and four piles of blankets and rugs that are used for sleeping but always rolled up during the day. Our host's wife sat next to a small metal burner near the door and poured boiling water from a kettle to make tea.

Pots and pans and several spoons and ladles, the kind the Chinese use for cooking, hung on nails. We haven't seen anyone using chopsticks to cook with, though in the past both Mongols and Chinese used them. This family had another tent for cooking, so we were spared the extra heat, but for most of the year, and even sometimes on summer evenings a fire is essential for warmth as well as for cooking.

On the table around which we sat (on the floor on handsome rugs) were the same foods that were on the table we had so recently left. Many forms and variations of cheese, butter, and yogurt; millet, cakes, cookies, and tea plus *kumiss*, a specialty of the Mongols. Made from fermented mare's milk, it is a strong, white, thick liquid that tastes bitter and sour as well as alcoholic. It is always brought out for guests and special occasions, and I find it almost impossible even to taste. Our host said to us as we sat down, "If you drink your kumiss *gambey* "bottoms up", my wife will sing for you. This is an old Mongolian custom." But it was not possible, so we never heard the beautiful woman's song.

Our host was a typical Mongol herdsman, fifty years old and looking much older. His face was deeply lined by years of exposure to the harsh Mongolian climate. But although he looked creased and wrinkled and his legs were bent from riding, he moved and acted like a young man. He wore a dal of heavy brown material and a brimmed felt hat, which he removed indoors. His wife wore the same kind of dress, but instead of a hat she wound a long piece of cloth around her head, tucking in the ends to make a turban. They were a handsome couple: red cheeks, brownish skin (hers was not wrinkled, though she was in her forties), black hair, and a natural ease and sophistication that people who live so close to nature often have. Mongols look very much like American Indians, though most of them are smaller; they have the same coloring and bone structure. They also wrap their babies tightly in blankets and carry them on their backs, the way our Indians used to.

Our host told us about his life before Liberation in 1949. He remembers the society of landlords and lamas, and poor peasants who were used and victimized and had no recourse. When he was growing up, a landlord could order a peasant girl to work in his house or to become a concubine, and death was the price of refusal. It is the same kind of story we are always told about the past: beatings and cruelty and people starving to death because whatever they had went to the landlord to pay the rent. It is the subject of revolutionary ballets and films and pictures and statues of peasant rebellions. Not hard for me to believe, but hard to believe it was so recent—less than thirty years ago.

We met three of his four children—taller than their parents, but with the same good looks and marvelous coloring.

After he had talked for a while, huge platters of boiled mutton were brought in. The fat is considered the best part, and a thick, yellowish layer surrounded the meat.

Harrison often tells about the time he was eating a meal with a family in Outer Mongolia and the specialty was a roasted lamb's head. His host plucked out the eye with a knife and offered it to him—the best part for the honored guest. Somehow he got it down, but his descriptions of the sensations are not appetizing.

I thought of this as our host, with a large hunting knife, began cutting huge slabs of the fat with just a bit of meat on each piece. But either he sensed my feelings or had been warned about effete foreigners, for he suggested that perhaps I didn't like fat as much as they did since I wasn't used to it, and gave me a small piece of meat alone.

Obviously there is no running water in a tent, and all the water for cooking, drinking, and washing has to be carried from the nearby well.

All the time we were sitting in the tent listening to our host, our Chinese companions were showing the effects of what they had been imbibing. They were constantly getting up to go out; the minute they returned and sat down, they dozed off; they were flushed and sweaty. And even our Mr. Mao looked sleepy and exhausted.

After a while we left the tent and just outside watched an exhibition of how horses are rounded up on the plains. More than one hundred horses of all ages and sizes were being herded by three or four riders. Each rider had a long pole with a rope lasso on the end. The horses were running fast, as if they were really wild. The riders raced along beside the herd, and when a man saw a horse he wanted, he galloped after it, got as close as he could, and threw the lasso over the horse's head. The rope tightened around the horse's neck, and the man played with the horse, almost as if he were playing with a fish, until the horse gave up. At that point he came in close, shortening the rope, and led the horse behind his own. It is a graceful art; there is not the roughness as with our cowboys lassoing animals and throwing them to the ground. The Mongol waits until the horse gives in.

This was an exhibit put on for our benefit, and I can't help but wonder how much herding of animals there really is these days. In Outer Mongolia the man and his horse seem much more a part of the real life than here, judging from what we have seen today.

From that we walked a few yards and sat in a semi-circle with about one hundred people, mostly Mongols, and watched a song and dance group. It was the strangest thing to find myself miles away from anywhere on this enormous, windy, hot, and dusty plain watching very talented people singing and dancing and playing music. This surely is an example of artists "going to the people", not to "learn" from them or to work with them but to entertain them and bring some pleasure and relief to people who in the old society would never have dreamed of anything like this. In addition, it is helpful in spreading propaganda about the glories of the Revolution, Mao, labor, and correct thinking.

Every province has a similar group, and they all do the same sort of dances and songs, with an emphasis on their own locality. So while today we saw the milkmaid dance and others we have seen before, there was a preponderance of strictly Mongolian specialties performed by Mongol artists.

We sat on the ground, and the musicians sat on straight-back wooden chairs in front of the jeep and truck they travel in. They wore brightly colored costumes and played on a combination of Western and Mongolian instruments, sometimes separately, sometimes in ensemble. After a while it didn't seem strange to be out on the plain in Central Asia listening to an orchestra made up of a cello, violin, clarinet, flute, oboe, accordion, xylophone, and several Mongolian violins and other stringed instruments that look like our banjo and ukulele.

All the performers were good, and there was a special festive feeling because of the surroundings. The best act was a Mongol dancer in bright blue trousers, scarlet tunic, and black boots who lept through the air higher than I have ever seen anyone leap, even in the best ballets.

Finally back here. H. is at a movie again, and I am really very comfortable now in this strange place. There is a rooster who cock-a-doodle-doos all day, and half the night strutting around the coal heap.

Thursday, September 8, 9:30 P.M.

TODAY WAS BETTER because I felt better. We started off early in the morning to visit a state livestock farm. Two jeeps, one ahead and one behind, and two ordinary cars made up our procession. For nearly two hours we jounced and bounced over roads, or no roads, just over the ground. Jeeps are built for such terrain, but every spring in the cars must have been broken. Certainly we were shaken around as if we were in one of those machines that stirs up paint.

This countryside is so like Outer Mongolia. Brown mountains encircle a huge area made of long, flat valleys in between smaller mountains and ranges of hills. The valleys stretch for miles; telephone or electric wires seem to run endlessly from nowhere to nowhere; only occasionally did we see a round white tent. Carts drawn by several horses, as many as five or six, were carrying heavy loads of stone, bricks, wood, food, and other supplies, back and forth from city to commune, commune to city. On the way home in the early evening many drivers had stopped, unharnessed and hobbled their horses, and were cooking supper over small fires. Every few miles two or three wagons were grouped together, for companionship and protection against the wind, which is always blowing.

The farm was in the fourth big valley. It covers an area of 3,330 square kilometers (1,286 square miles) and has a population of over 11,000. The Chinese (Han) population numbers 9,300, and the remaining 2,100 are Mongols and other minorities. Out of the total population, 5,261 are staff members, and 221 are cadres; the rest are family members. A total of 1,100 educated youth, meaning high school graduates, have settled here. Some are children of the original workers, some have been sent from Peking. In the leading body of this farm there are six chairmen: four Mongol, one Han, and one Manchu. The very top head man came from another state farm in Silinhot. (There are more than twenty state farms in this region of Inner Mongolia.)

There are eleven branch farms, five totally engaged in animal husbandry, four in animal agriculture, and two in agriculture alone. Thirteen units are engaged in industry and other work related to general farm needs—wool, textiles, farm machinery, rug making (by hand), cement, a brick kiln, pharmaceutical factories, food production, water conservancy, and transportation. They say they are basically mechanized and use tractors, trucks, and combines on the large vegetable fields and grasslands. They use hand tractors on smaller areas.

They have 153,000 animals including sheep, horses, cattle, camels, and donkeys and have been just about self-sufficient in fodder, grain, and feed for the last two years.

The layout of the buildings at the Farm Headquarters was similar to that of the commune yesterday. The table in the reception room was a welcome change from yesterday. Two cloths were thumbtacked together on the table, and on it were millet, two kinds of butter, cheeses, and some real tea as well as a glass of the special Mongolian tea. We sat down for the usual briefing, during which all the men who were with us yesterday kept leaving to go to the toilet. Many of them were sick; all had hangovers. Mr. Mao is very ill, and we don't know what to do about him. He has a history of ulcers, and on top of all the heavy food he stayed up too late talking and drinking, which he shouldn't do. He looks terrible.

We visited a backyard blast furnace, which was like a Rube Goldberg arrangement, a workshop where indoor electrical convertors are made, Then on to the hospital which was clean and neat and seemed pretty well equipped considering the circumstances. At the rug factory, girls were weaving blue and brown rugs by hand, the way I have seen them in Sikkim. They are used mostly on the floors of tents.

We went next to a building with several rooms with beds for a rest before lunch. Except for the beds, it looked more like a building for animals than for people. Floors were of stone, walls of stucco, and a little stove was in the corner of each room with a sort of trough for ashes that emptied out into the corridor. There were about four rooms in our building, which was at right angles to the room where we had lunch.

We both had to go to the toilet, but I said I couldn't go through an experience like yesterday's again. We wondered what to do. I could use the spittoon, which is omnipresent and like a potty, and put the result in the stove. But we decided I'd be found out, for it would trickle out into the corridor. There was no alternative, so we set out together. As we started off, the Mongol girl who is with us came behind and accompanied me after H. and I had to go our separate ways. Unlike yesterday, she didn't wait outside but came in with me. This place was bigger, four holes instead of two, and far worse, with some dead birds mixed up with the expected mess. I hesitated a moment, but again there was no alternative. We unbuttoned ourselves, went to adjoining holes, and relieved ourselves together. Very friendly, as the Chinese are always saying.

To find such filth and lack of hygiene in even this remote part of China seems extraordinary to me. I see no reason why the trenches are not cleaned out daily. There are certainly enough people who aren't terribly busy who could do it. I should think diseases would be prevalent. Their inoculations must be powerful. Where are the members of the Revolutionary Committees and cadres trained in Peking to keep order?

Back in the room where we rested, a smiling young man brought us a thermos of hot water, two basins, fresh soap, a towel, and a kettle. I was touched. Though the room looked like a cow barn, there were two beds with quilts, and each had one of those strange pillows that feel like the bean bags of my childhood. When I asked what they were made of, Mr. Mao said, "Beans." They are Chinese pillows, not Mongolian, and we first encountered them in Yenan in 1972. They are usually at the foot of the bed when the bed is made up.

The smiling young man carried my tea for me to lunch, where we sat at two round tables. Harrison's and my presence at our table curtailed the drinking a little, but our influence did not extend to the other table, where even the drivers were swilling *mao tai*. They say that drivers never drink when they expect to drive, but that was not the case today.

The food was nicely prepared and cooked by a genial cook, four girl assistants in white coats, and two men. The dishes were boiled mutton and lovely mushrooms with meat and green peppers. The peppers are delicious. String beans and garlic, hot peppers finely sliced, sea slugs (ugh!) in the three-delicacies dish, gelatinous mushrooms, eggplant and garlic, all very oily, followed one after the other. Dumplings of mutton were served with whole cloves of raw garlic; other dishes were flavored with long, thin strips of desert vegetables.

The soup was wonderful with tiny dumplings, mushrooms, and very fine Chinese noodles. A new experience was candied hard-boiled eggs, sometimes whole, sometimes the yolks and whites served separately. The rice is much coarser than in Peking. Cucumbers were sliced with the skin on, as big as I remember them in Sikkim, where we likened them to baseball bats.

The platters kept coming and coming, finally ending up with quantities of cookies and cakes and little puffballs of bean paste covered with sugar made in the shape of a sheep's head.

There was much drinking and toasting, belching and smacking of lips, absolutely revolting. Our host here is a very vulgar man, a Chinese who has been here twenty-seven years. He seems to have lost the good qualities of the Chinese and acquired the bad ones of the Mongols. He is big and coarse and a smart aleck. He keeps grabbing our cameras and taking pictures of us. He drinks a great deal at meals and urges everyone else to *gambey*. He is the only Chinese I have ever met who offends me. The comrade from Huhehot is better behaved today, but not much.

After lunch we returned to the cowshed and lay down together on a tiny single bed and talked about the Mongols and what has happened to them. It is the mix that doesn't appeal to me—the heavy hand of Russia in Outer Mongolia, the less heavy, but just as insistent, Chinese influence here, pushing their way of life on proud nomadic people. I know industrialization is inevitable, but it doesn't suit everyone. I feel sad up here. It reminds me of how I felt when I went to Bangkok in 1966 and the American presence was so strong it was smothering the special Oriental qualities of the Thais.

We had said that one half hour's rest would be enough for us, and everyone nodded and acquiesced, but they were all still asleep after one hour had passed. So we didn't get going in our two cars and two jeeps until nearly 3:00 P.M. We took off, going northeast, right over the plains, sometimes on wheel tracks, more often just on the grass. We went for miles; H. and I and Mr. Mao were in back, and our big host was in front. Neither he nor the driver had ever been to where we were going, and I began to worry that it would be dark before we turned homeward and we would have a three-hour drive on the Mongolian steppe with no roads, no lights, and no one who knew where we were going. The suite in the guest house began to look mightily attractive.

At last we came upon a herd of horses with three herdsmen keeping them together. They were beautiful, all mares and colts of different sizes and ages. The Chinese are breeding thoroughbreds and other larger horses to the Mongolian horses to get a bigger, stronger horse. Most of these were black, shiny, and healthy looking. They will be used for agriculture, carting, and with animal herds. In the old days the Chinese went in for horse racing in a big way; perhaps that will come back.

We got out and watched the horses, and they watched us. They were friendly and curious and not a bit afraid.

Then back into the cars and jeeps, over the plain, a sharp turn to go up over a high jagged hill and down the other side. There we found a herd of "yellow sheep," tended by one man. They are enormous rams with huge curved horns, and testicles hanging down to the ground. I don't see how they can move with those great things swinging about. We got out, admired the sheep, felt the wool, and that was it, thank heaven.

We headed back to Silinhot, taking a different route. I can't really say *road*, because so often there wasn't one.

Down into a dry riverbed where the sand was a foot thick (and I don't understand why we didn't get stuck), across to the other side, back onto the plain, bumpety bump. Our driver went terribly fast, and my heart was in my mouth; also my head banged on the top of the car occasionally.

Suddenly we stopped; the car was too hot, it was boiling over. We got out; our Chinese and Mongol traveling companions got out of the other car, and we got into it to sit, because it was so dusty and windy. Our car was turned around so that the wind blew on the engine to cool if off. It didn't work. We continued on in the other car while our driver went to a small settlement nearby to get some water.

The new driver drove more slowly, and we got back about 6:00 P.M. relieved if exhausted. There was hot water, boiling in fact. We each had a bath and ate supper peacefully alone at our big table separated from our hosts and Mr. Mao by the usual series of screens.

There was a terrible dust storm, but a movie was scheduled. H. was a good sport and went, but I pleaded "advanced age," as they are always saying, and stayed in.

One of the funniest mix-ups with translation occurred today. I understood that there was quite a "semen" operation, and it seemed reasonable on such a huge farm to have artificial insemination. But I was mystified at the referrals to a semen factory. And when we drove by a fairly large brick building and were told that it was the semen factory, I said to Harrison, "For heaven's sake, why do they have such a big building? All they need is a bull and a container, maybe a cow to interest him." It turned out this was the cement factory.

It is of interest that in the buildings we have visited up here almost every door has a padlock, and bars cover many windows. We don't know if this was true in Inner Mongolia five years ago, but it certainly wasn't in the places we went to then. It must be the result of the disruption and anarchy promoted by the Gang.

Friday, September 9,
Huhehot, Inner Mongolia

THIS MORNING at Silinhot we went first to the Research
Center, which devotes its efforts to improving the pasture
grasses and experimenting with seeds from all over the
world, crossing them with the native grasses, etc. The
head man is a Mongol, but the head research man is
Chinese, and not attractive. He gave us an unusually long
political blast, which our big host twice interrupted,
telling him to cut it out and get down to the business of
grasses and what they do there.

They really have done wonders. We saw closely
planted rows of trees, which were being irrigated as we
walked by. The water comes from underground wells.
Protected by the trees and walls are many patches of
various grasses, clover, and alfalfa—some from Canada,
the United States, and other countries. These patches are
grown from seed in order to produce more seed to be
mixed and experimented with, crossed with native
grasses, etc. To my eternal question about the ad-
visability of plowing up large areas of grasslands and
creating dustbowls, they said they had learned from ex-

perience and from their mistakes. Only moist areas and places that are protected either by mountains or planted windbreaks or walls should be plowed. Considering what they began with and what they have to contend with (weather, old customs dying hard), they have made enormous progress.

We saw the laboratory where they test the nourishment value of the grasses and saw examples of what they have grown—grasses and grains four or five times as big as the native species.

I asked about the pretty purple flower we had seen in Taching, and no one could tell me what it is. Suddenly I saw some growing; we stopped the car, and I dashed out to pick a piece. It is called phoenix. It is not a real grass, looks a little like a thistle. The cows like it, but it has no nourishment.

We visited the cookie factory, where we were shown around by the head man, a very nice Mongol. We had to wear white coats for our tour, like hospital workers. As we walked out into the really good, dry air and smelled cookies baking, I said how lovely it smelled, and the man said, "You seem very happy." Well, I was, to be smelling such nice smells as this morning—hay and baking. A welcome change from some of the unattractive odors we have encountered recently.

The cookie factory has five workshops, one each for cookies, biscuits, candy, fermenting, and beer. It has a staff of 127 workers, 22 of whom are national minorities (which represents only a small percentage), and 37 percent are women.

Special cakes and cookies were being baked for the Moon Ceremony, on September 21, and they tasted delicious right out of the oven, not as hard as the cookies on our table in the dining room. Cookies that look like *petits-beurres* were also better hot.

The oven was brick and about forty feet long. The cookies went in at one end on a conveyor belt, and in three minutes came out baked. They continued on conveyor belts for culling and sorting and ended up in what looked like huge piles on the floor, though I imagine they were bins. It was a cheerful place to go through and seemed efficient and clean according to standards up here.

From our window in the guest house we could see the roofs of the lamasary H. had seen on our first day at Silinhot, when I had stayed in bed. This morning we got closer, and it is a sad sight. Unless you have seen something like this with your own eyes, it is hard to imagine, or believe, what has happened.

The old walls are just banged out in some places; crude walls of wood and glass enclose some of the formerly beautiful courtyards and open rooms; chickens scratch in the dusty ground, and pigs roam at will. Many people must live in it now, and I wouldn't like to see the inside of any part. Several big healthy trees grow in the erstwhile courtyards, protected for years by the high red walls.

They said it wasn't an important lamasary, so there was no point in preserving it. Perhaps it is natural. Why should anyone feel like preserving symbols of their exploitation? Life was wretched for the peasants and ordinary people in those days, and it is still too close. But it is too bad.

We flew here to Huhehot at about 11:30 this morning. Huhehot means "green city," and it certainly looks it, both from the air and on the ground. It is an oasis in this brown, dusty area. Protected by the Taching mountain range, it is less windy and warmer than Silinhot, though still high. Colorado Springs and its surrounding area could look like this if it were irrigated and devoted to agriculture.

A tall, pleasant Chinese man, Mr. Chang Shan-kung, met us and has accompanied us everywhere. We had a nice, slow drive into the city along roads lined with trees. This is a real city up here in the boondocks.

We are staying in a guest house that used to be the consulate of Outer Mongolia until they cleared out along with the Russians in 1960. It is a long building of two or three stories, higher in the middle. We have a big, sunny room with a double bed and a single bed, plus a fat brown leather sofa and two matching chairs that might have come out of a landlord's house. On the table is an embossed silver tray with an ashtray, a match box stand, and a cigarette box, all in silver, the last having horses hammered out in relief all around it.

We had lunch in a dining room by ourselves. The food was light and good, but I scarcely ate anything.

After a nap we drove in a procession of four cars through an air raid shelter tunnel for *twenty-five minutes*, emerging at the foot of Taching Mountain. It is a typical sharp Chinese mountain, part of the range that protects the city. It was nice to look across the river, dry now, and see some houses within high walls, and trees and flowers growing thickly. A factory smokestack is right behind, belching out black smoke, but I didn't see that until we left and were some distance away.

From there we went to a shelter near the airport. We walked through a guerilla post tunnel, in which a definite force can attack invading troops landing at the airport. We walked up into a pillbox that had five or six openings for shooting through. Hearing a lot of giggling, I turned to look out the window behind me and met a hundred eyes in fascinated faces staring at us. I poked H., who turned around and said, "Boo," in a loud voice, whereupon they fled, giggling and laughing, but were back again in a few minutes. At one point in the shelter they handed me a telephone, and I said *"Nehow"* —"hello" in Chinese—to a voice on the other end. When we got to one of the posts, the girl to whom I had spoken was there on duty, and it was the reason for a lot of talking and laughing.

That was the afternoon's activities. We returned to our big, comfortable room with its clean rugs but not a clean bathtub. H. played billiards on the big table in the hall, and I rested and washed. We had dinner alone again. The screen shielding the kitchen door must also have come from a landlord's house. It is of dark carved wood on both ends and red silk panels with gold calligraphy and birds, very ornate.

Dinner was good, and I felt much better. Afterward we met the real boss of the area, a most attractive

Mongol, Mr. Ba. He took us to a big barnlike theater with hard seats, crammed with Chinese and Mongols.

As today is the anniversary of Mao's death, this was a memorial performance. All acts were announced in a deep bass voice by a young Mongol who wore a bright blue *dal* and excessive makeup. They were repeated in a high, shrill monotone by a doll-like Chinese girl. She wore the regulation gray suit Chinese women wear, with the jacket too short, not very becoming.

First we heard "The East Is Red," played by an orchestra with a Mongol conductor. It was louder than anything I've ever heard in a concert hall, and no shading of sound, all a huge blast. A girl with a remarkably pleasant voice sang a poem Mao had written to his second wife. It was banned for ten years by Chiang Ching. The audience talked the whole time, and only the strongest voice or tone could be heard above the noise. Maybe that's why the music and singing are so loud.

There were several songs and recitations and a very cute dance showing a young couple making some soup and giving it to Chairman Mao, whose light was burning all night because he was working so hard. I said to Harrison, "This is really a children's society, isn't it?" and he said, "Yes, they couldn't keep it together without making Mao into this hero." All the songs and dances were dedicated to him or were about him. In the present everyday life Chairman Hua is carrying on the great tradition, but I don't believe anyone can step into a folk hero's shoes.

I came home during the intermission as planned, so as

not to get overtired. My escort was the Chinese man who first met us at the airport here and accompanied us to Silinhot. While there he was rowdy and crude; here he is a paragon of good behavior. At the guest house I found that there was not a drop of water in any tap or in the toilet. It was a desperate discovery, with Harrison and Mr. Mao still at the theater and no one else in sight. I didn't know what to do. I tried the public women's toilet across the hall, but other people must have had the same idea. It was worse than the Silinhot outhouse.

I left a note for H. and slid it under the door into the hall so he and Mr. Mao would see it before Mr. M. retired. I wrote, "I can't get through the night like this." Poor Mr. Mao, to have to deal with this crisis after a relaxing evening at the theater. Everyone was asleep or had gone home, and the controls were under lock and key. He came back with the news that the pipes were broken and there would be no water. But a boy appeared with extra thermos jugs, and Mr. Mao and he miraculously found two full pails of water. So we were saved.

Saturday, September 10, Huhehot, 8:00 A.M.

PROMPTLY AT SEVEN this morning, the water went on, as good as new. Mr. Mao had also suggested that it was turned off because water was piped to the countryside at night, but I didn't believe that any more than that the pipes were broken. They simply turned the water off at night, and that was that. Peculiar when people are staying in the guest house.

Because I came home during the intermission last night, I missed seeing Modegema dance. (She is the Mongolia lady Mr. Mao met on the airplane.) I hadn't realized she was to perform and would gladly have risked being sick again just to have seen her. Harrison said she was wonderful. She danced what I have always thought of as a gypsy dance, wiggling and rippling her torso and arms, all with bowls on her head and wine cups in her hands. The audience was ecstatic and gave her an ovation.

The same day, at the Min Zu Hotel,
Peking, 5 P.M.

WHAT A LONG day!! We began with a visit to the university at Huhehot this morning. It is a general university of arts and letters, science and technology. The main object is to train scientists and technicians to promote socialism in Inner Mongolia. Education must serve the political purpose set down by Chairman Mao, they told us.

It is a small university, started in October 1957. The curriculum includes Chinese (Han) language and literature, Mongolian language and literature, politics and history, philosophy and history, foreign languages, mathematics, physics, chemistry, botany, and zoology. There is a physical-culture department. They do research in Mongolian and Han languages and in Marxism and Leninism. Originally the course was for five years; now, according to Mao's instructions, it is for only three. Approximately 3,500 students have been trained here; all have been assigned to autonomous regions. Presently there are 500 students, though the capacity is 1,500. A total of 350 graduated last year.

Five factories are attached to the university —electronic, chemical, engineering, computer, and pharmaceutical. It runs a farm, a printing house, and there is a school journal. Students are selected from workers' communes. Most are advanced workers. They have had practical experience, so they come here mainly to learn theory in the factory and countryside. They will learn military affairs, agriculture, and industry in addition to the regular studies. Science and technical students work in the factories along with the teacher. The university has recovered from the undermining of quality by the Gang of Four, they said. Education has been transformed, and students are enthusiastic about carrying out the socialist line. A niece of Chou En-lai is a student here. She will finish her studies and then go and live with the herdspeople and carry the socialist way to those who have not yet been indoctrinated.

Here are some notes I wrote at the meeting with the university people:

H. When will the new students be enrolled, and how many?
A. The Conference on Education is being held at the Ministry of Information in Peking now—they will decide.
H. Was this university closed down during the Cultural Revolution?
A. Yes, for three or four years.
H. When did it resume?
A. 1971.
H. How many students enrolled then?
A. One hundred students.
H. How many members of the faculty are here now who were here ten years ago?
A. Most of the seven hundred staff are here now; only a few were transferred to other places because of their families.
H. Has it been necessary to eliminate any faculty because of association with Liu Shao-chi, Lin Piao, or the Gang of Four?

A. Only a few.

H. Can you give me an example?

A. Someone with a wrong attitude was sent to a farm.

H. Can you give me a particular example?

A. A teacher of Mongolian language openly advocated splitting the union of nationalities. He was punished according to law, was sent to a labor farm for several years. Now he has returned to the university. He has changed. [He is assigned to "certain work," which means not teaching but doing administration work. *Splitting* and *factionalism* refers to taking the Mongolian line, wanting Mongols to remain Mongolian and not be under Chinese influence.]

H. Do you have an example of someone more connected with those three elements—Liu Shao-chi, Lin Piao, and the Gang—not just nationalism?

A. Another professor on the faculty of the Han language department had some connections with the Gang. He opposed the Central Committee; he took a stand with the Gang, did many evil things. We exposed him and criticized him.

H. Could I have an example of one of his crimes?

A. He wrote to the Gang of Four criticizing Hua.

H. How did you find out about that?

A. He threw away the draft letter; it was found by a colleague.

H. What became of him?

A. He was arrested according to law.

H. How was he punished?

A. He has not been punished yet. He has confessed.

His punishment will be according to his attitude.

H. Were there any others like this man?

A. Only a few.

H. I never know what is meant by "a few."

A. Only three.

H. Where are they?

A. Still in the university.

H. How about students?

A. None. Also, the Revolutionary Committee in this university had nothing to do with the Gang.

H. How is discipline among the students now?

A. Since the smashing of the Gang, they observe it well.

H. Does that mean that before the smashing they didn't?

A. They were influenced by the Gang.

H. How?

A. Mainly they wouldn't listen to cadres or teachers. They behaved according to their own wishes, and some went out to make contact with other factions—a sort of anarchism.

H. We have heard that students haven't studied much during the last few years. Is that true?

A. Most students here behaved quite well.

H. Do you have any scholarly contact with other universities in China or other countries?

A. So far no contact.

H. Before cooling of relations, was there any contact with the People's Republic of Mongolia [Outer Mongolia]?

A. There was a cultural agreement then—contact mainly centered on Mongolian-language teaching.

Two language experts were here.

H. Do your teachers attend conferences held all over the world on Mongolian culture, literature, language?

A. No.

H. Do you receive or exchange publications on Mongolian studies?

A. So far, no exchange on scientific research. Sometimes we receive publications indirectly from Outer Mongolia and through other friends.

H. Have you received any foreign visitors—Owen Lattimore, for instance?

A. In recent years only Lattimore.

H. Is that a policy, to have no contact?

A. It is not a policy. We should learn from foreigners. So far we don't know about other countries. The Gang of Four didn't approve. That is not Chairman Mao's principle.

H. I am a member of a Mongolian society in the United States that would be delighted to send journals, have exchange, send experts here.

A. We would welcome that. [Not convincing to me!]

H. Is there interest in Mongolian language among students who are not Mongols?

A. Yes. I'll give you an example. Premier Chou's niece, Chou Pin-chien, has been here two years studying Mongol.

H. How long has she been in Inner Mongolia altogether?

A. She graduated from high school in 1971 and went to Silinhot to do physical labor with the herdsmen.

She will graduate in one year. Students are encouraged to learn both languages.

H. What work does she hope to do?

A. The work will be assigned by the party committee.

H. How old is she?

A. Twenty-four.

H. Will it be possible to meet some students?

A. Yes, it has been arranged.

We saw students in their classrooms, including Chou En-lai's niece, but we had no discussion.

During our tour of the library I noticed a photocopy of *Scientific American* on the shelf. Harrison took a picture of me holding it, and we will give it to Gerry Piel, the publisher, so he can see how far his magazine travels, even if illegitimately. The library is where they carry on the research on the Mongolian language and dialects. It was well stocked with appropriate books, and we met several professors as well as the head librarian.

We had a drive around the city. It is like a European provincial city, with paved streets, conventional buildings, and lots of trees. It is very green. Traffic is constant and heavy, made up of many carts and wagons pulled by horses, bicycles, trucks, but very few cars. Here two people are allowed to ride on the same bicycle; in Peking and most other cities it is forbidden.

Mr. Ba gave us a lunch back at the guest house. There were many marvelous dishes as always. A surprise was a "friendship" cake, a real cake with soft frosting. With it we had a fruit compote of apricots lichis, and pineapple.

I said to our host that I didn't believe the landlords had had such wonderful food, and he answered, "No, they were not civilized."

I couldn't help but contrast the behavior today of the comrade who accompanied us to Silinhot to his behavior at the two lunches there. At both of the latter he got drunk and sloppy and unattractive. Today, under the influence of the gentlemanly Mongol, he was quiet and polite.

After a short rest we flew back here to Peking at 1:30 P.M. It was a good day to see the valleys and mountains and all the farming, as well as the Great Wall and Ming Tombs. They are so definitely defined by trees and the shape and plans of the tombs, it is easy to spot them from the air. Looking down from the airplane I imagined all the wonderful treasures buried there—it is a thrilling thought.

Here, back in our old room at the Min Zu, it is very nice. I have washed everything including my hair, and H. is writing a story, just like after all our other trips. We are taking Frank and Ruth Coe out for dinner; the Adlers can't come, unfortunately.

Later

WE MET THE Coes at the Chin Yang restaurant. Chin Yang is a mountain in Shansi province, and this restaurant specializes in Shansi cooking. The building was a warlord's or a very rich man's house and has not been altered or gussied up in becoming a restaurant. We had a small private dining room with a sofa, an armchair, and a round table, big enough for eight or ten. We drank tea for awhile and then had another wonderful meal, though neither Frank nor I ate much. I am learning at last how to get through a Chinese dinner—take only a tiny bit of each dish.

We began with hors d'oeuvres—a platter of plain boiled shrimp, slices of pork, candied walnuts, minute slices of fried fish, finely sliced cucumbers, and noodles. A profusion of dishes followed, including a slimy concoction of shark's fins, soybeans and tiny onions in sauce, and special Shansi duck. Many Chinese prefer this to Peking duck. It is thoroughly roasted and crisp and has practically no fat. The waitress brought it in on a platter and lightly pushed it down with a fork. It collapsed and split, so we could help ourselves to small pieces easily. It is served with thin, hollow wheat biscuits, a little like popovers, much more delicate than the buns that come with Peking duck; tiny strips of onion and bean sauce for dipping in, like Peking duck; and thick, flakey wheat cakes.

After that came mushrooms and bamboo in white sauce, a very good clear soup, and apples for dessert. All through dinner we had white wine, which was good and cold, cold beer, and Laoshan mineral water, which we can't live without.

We talked, as always on this trip no matter with whom we're talking, about the Gang of Four. How they got so powerful, how Mao must have been mixed up in it

137

(which we can't say to a Chinese)—the Gang of Five, some people say. I asked Ruth about how the workers reacted to the Gang, how many must have been influenced and followed their road, and now, since the smashing, what do they think? And what is thought of them by the people on top now? She said the workers are never blamed. It is recognized that they are manipulated—no, she didn't say that, that's *my* term —she said the workers can be used and persuaded to think thus and so, but everyone knows it's the higher-ups who do the damage. They are the guilty ones.

We talked about how difficult it is to create a society in which everyone does have an equal chance, how an elite is bound to emerge. What can be done about it? Can people be regulated so as to prevent some from rising to the top or taking advantage of others? Can the desire or craving for power be curtailed? The Soviet Union harasses, imprisons, and exiles her intellectual freethinking elite, but the proletariat has created an elite of its own. The son of a Russian dissident living in the United States now was asked where he went to school in Russia, and he answered, "To the school for the elite, naturally." Constant revolution may prevent such a development, but it also prevents progress in all fields.

H. is calling up his story. I can never get over the idea of picking up the telephone halfway around the world and dictating a story to the *New York Times*. It is a nice story about Madame Soong. He is going to ask the *Times* to call the family, say we're okay and will be home the twentieth, or thereabouts.

Sunday, September 11, at the Peking airport
for the seventh time, 3:30 P.M.

I WOULDN'T HAVE thought such a thing possible, or even probable. Five years ago we waited at this airport all day for the plane to Shanghai, and finally it was canceled, and we went back to the hotel. We flew there the next day. That time they said it was the weather, but we found out later it was something wrong with the radar apparatus.

Today, five years later, we have been here all day, too, since 9:30 this morning, and the plane has just been canceled. A taxi has been called, and now we are waiting for our bags, which we have to drag all the way back to the hotel.

We thought we were to fly at 11:00 A.M., so we left the hotel at around 9:30. We were having a leisurely breakfast a little after 8:00 when I saw Mr. Mao appear, looking like a ghost, and sit down at the desk in the dining room [of the Min Zu Hotel]. He looked as if he had no strength. We didn't think about the time, we were just worrying about him, when he staggered over and said we should leave in ten minutes, because the plane was to fly at ten.

So off we went. Mr. Mao said he had terrible stomach trouble and a headache and was dizzy. He slept most of the way to the airport and didn't object when Harrison and I carried all our bags. We had everything with us because we are not coming back to Peking this time. We got everything shipped off and have been reading and writing in the waiting room ever since, except for two brief visits to the restaurant. Mr. Mao accompanied us, and while we were having just a cup of coffee, he had porridge and dark pickled vegetables on his poor upset stomach. No wonder he is sick. But for lunch he had just a drop of soup and a drop of tea.

The clinic at the airport was closed, so he couldn't get any pills or any medical help. I gave him some Bufferin. We are worried to death about him because he has had an ulcer, though he says it was cured. He has been under a strain having to translate all the time, and the life of the Mongols is not for him. They, and the Chinese up there, are tough, hard-drinking people, and they kept him up every night until one o'clock talking and drinking, and certainly at meals they poured down the *mao tai* and urged him to join them. The food was heavy and greasy, and he ate too much. All the things we watch out for when traveling—fatigue, overeating, and drinking.

Later, back in Room 501, Min Zu Hotel, 8:00 P.M.

WE GOT BACK here at about 5:00 P.M. and haven't seen Mr. Mao since. Mr. Liu came to see us and said Mr. Mao

140

was asleep and that he thought he'd be all right in the morning. Mr. Liu said we'd be taken care of in Shanghai, not to worry. We're not worrying about ourselves, only about poor Mr. Mao. We think he should have a doctor and stay in bed or go to the hospital.

Harrison has a cold and irritated nose and throat from the dust and wind, I am not back to normal yet, and our companion is down and out. So much for Mongolia.

A prominent black American journalist and columnist and a group of ten other writers and teachers, three whites among them, were here when we got back from Mongolia, and we met them in the hall. I rode up in the elevator with a terribly nice man who said his wife had read my other book on China and the advice about traveling light, but still brought too much. I said I had too!

We were looking forward to seeing them at breakfast the next morning but learned that at 10:00 P.M., when most Chinese are asleep, they had moved, lock, stock, and barrel, to the Peking Hotel. They had announced on arrival at the airport that they expected to stay at the Peking Hotel. (They couldn't have spent much time in communist countries, because one always goes where one is sent—there is never any choice.) I suppose it has more status than the Min Zu, and perhaps, being black, they thought they were being discriminated against. We telephoned to say we'd missed them.

Now to bed, and we'll hope for better luck all around tomorrow. We are to leave the hotel at 7:20 A.M. and fly at 8:45. That's the plan anyway.

Monday, September 12, almost to Shanghai on the plane, 10:45 A.M.

SO FAR, so good. We got up at 6:00 A.M., had some coffee, packed up again, and went down to breakfast.
Everyone was sleep: The boy on our floor was still rolled
up in his quilt on the sofa near the desk, the doors to the
TV room were shut, and the rest of the staff must have
been in there sleeping on those sofas. The elevator was
running, but downstairs the dining room doors were
closed, though not locked.

We walked in; two men were rolled in their quilts on
the floor, and there was no one else around. However,
news spreads quickly in this country, if they want it to,
and soon our familiar dining room man came. We were
ushered to a table, and in a short time had a very nice
breakfast of canned lichis, eggs and ham, toast, and coffee—all good and hot.

Mr. Mao appeared looking cheerful and very different
from yesterday. He said he felt okay. Maybe he does, but
he is still pale and weak. In the taxi to the airport I said I
had some "suggestions to make," which is what we are
often asked to do, and number one is that foreign guests

should not be subjected to the customs of the Mongols or to the vulgarity of men like our Chinese host in Silinhot. Mr. Mao said that he had made three suggestions when he was there: (1) that they make more toilets; (2) that they don't give guests so much to eat, and especially so much meat, and (3) that they don't drink so much and urge or force guests to. Of course they don't succeed in forcing us to eat or drink, but it's unattractive to have to sit there watching them.

Just about to land at Shangai airport

IT'S THICKLY overcast. The rivers, canals, lakes, and ponds look as if they were overflowing, and the countryside is emerald green.

Still Monday, September 12, at the Ching Chin Hotel, 8 P.M.

AS SOON AS we landed, we learned that a typhoon struck here three days ago and raged for two days. So that is the reason for our delayed flight. Great trees are uprooted and resting on houses, fences, and each other. Those that fell on the streets have been sawed off or removed already. They say there was no other damage either to buildings or people and that no lives were lost. It must have been a terrible wind.

We are in a lovely hotel that was built by the British.

The bellboys wear white uniforms, are polite and agreeable, and act like trained hotel personel. The boy on our floor came all the way up to the dining room with us to be sure we found it and that we got the table reserved for us and were given the proper attention. Our room is finished in dark polished wood. The bathroom is heaven compared with some we have had recently; no hole has been cut in the floor, and it is spotless. From our windows we see the building where Nixon and Kissinger stayed and the lawn where Kissinger announced the signing of the Shanghai Communiqué.

After lunch and a rest in our comfortable room we went to a machine tool factory. It employs 6,000 people, 1,300 of them women, 900 cadres. There are ten workshops; one is a full-time technical school. Before Liberation they made farm tools such as simple hoes. Now they turn out first-class, sophisticated tools that are used for working with steel. Before going into a precision-grinding workshop we had to take off our shoes and put on slippers, as if we were entering a Buddhist temple. Harrison was impressed with the quality of the products.

While we were being briefed at the factory, I took these notes:

We have in this reception room the director of the factory; Mr. Mao, who is only half here; our new interpreter, who is charming but not as good as Mr. Mao; the man who is our host in Shanghai; and a violent young man who gets angry and agitated at almost every question. Quite often they are arguing and shouting at each other, and it seems very difficult to get anything straight. H. is plowing through, and I wish he would finish so that Mr. Mao can get to a doctor. Mr. Mao must wish so, too.

(A few days after this, when Mr. Mao was back to normal, I said to him, "I should think sometimes you must get so tired of us asking all these questions and it taking so long to get satisfactory answers, especially when you weren't feeling well, that you would not repeat everything just the way it is said and get it all over with quicker."

He was thoroughly shocked and replied with fervor, "Of course not. An enterpreter's job is to interpret every word exactly as it is said."

I felt a little ashamed at having such a dishonorable thought and think he showed great fortitude.)

The head man is very nice looking, but it seems to me he is giving H. a lot of political crap. He is head of the executive office of the Revolutionary Committee, so his job is to be liaison between Revolutionary Committee and workers. He came here in 1953 as an apprentice for three years. For five years he was a worker, for two years more he did technical work, and after that he became a cadre, which means party worker. In 1957 Chairman Mao came here personally, and they keep bringing that up.

I tried to keep track of the questions and answers, and here are some:

H. Did the workers play a role in the Cultural Revolution?

A. The Cultural Revolution was initiated by Chairman Mao. The workers were the main force.

H. What role did workers in this factory play?

A. When workers here realized that Chairman Mao had initiated the Cultural Revolution, they revolted against the revisionist line and seized the power of the capitalist roaders in this factory and set up the Revolutionary Committee.

H. What was the date?

A. July 8, 1967, the tenth anniversary of Chairman Mao's visit here. The workers seized power from the capitalists on that date and purified staff and workers. On that basis they organized the party committee in November 1969.

H. Does that mean that on July 8, 1967, the heads here were thrown out?

A. Only a few.

H. How about the director? [Much talking and arguing among themselves.]

A. Originally fourteen members of the Revolutionary Committee.

H. What happened to the director?

A. In 1966 the director of this factory was sent to the interior to be in charge of another factory, so there was no director. That man is still in charge of that other factory, in Sian. The assistant director was not included in the Revolutionary Committee because he went the revisionist line. But later he changed and now is vice-chairman of the Revolutionary Committee.

H. Are the original fourteen members still members of the Revolutionary Committee?

A. Only one is not.

H. Did the factory workers participate in the Cultural Revolution?

A. Wang Hung-wen [youngest member of the Gang of Four] came here. As head of the Textile Workers' Union he was welcomed.

H. No one here thought that their leaders were on the wrong track, did they?

A. At that time Chairman Mao supported Wang. We learned about the Gang of Four bit by bit.

H. Isn't it true that workers in this factory played a leading role in the Cultural Revolution and in the January Uprising (the big Shanghai uprising in January 1967)?

A. Yes, you're right.

H. When did the workers, or our host, begin to feel that something was wrong?

A. In our factory the Tenth National Congress was not according to Chairman Mao's instructions. In 1974, during the time of criticizing Lin Piao and Confucius, more than seventy cadres in our factory were attacked.

[Here the violent young man became agitated and talked so fast that no one could understand him, and I lost the thread except to learn that the Gang had sung another tune and criticized Teng Hsiao-ping and that there was an attack on Chou En-lai, and Mao learned of this and criticized the people who had instigated the attack.]

H. It seems strange to me that although no one wanted to, they went along with the Gang.

[Harrison kept asking why people didn't question

what was happening, especially the cadres. There seems to be no answer. I would guess that the cadres were playing both sides, or not playing either, hoping to be on the winning team whichever it was. A matter of survival, not necessarily ideology.

The Shanghai branch of the Gang of Four, because they did not trust the regular army, had organized a special private army of one million, referred to as the militia. Large quantities of rifles and amunition were amassed for their use.]

H. Did the workers join the militia?

A. No.

H. What happened to the rifles?

A. They were put in special places.

H. Where are they now?

A. Still in those places.

To his question of how many people in this factory lost their positions or are being subjected to criticism, the answer was, "In our factory only one member is under investigation." Which seems strange when we have just heard that many people went along with the Gang because they thought the Gang represented Mao's thoughts.

We didn't get back from the factory until 6:15 P.M., had a quick supper, then H. went off to a concert. I declined again, because of my "advanced age." The Chinese invented that term for us, and there are times when I feel like taking advantage of it, such as now. I would like to hear the concert, but I am just too weary. We got up at 6:00 A.M. in Peking and have been going

148

pretty much all the time since then. We are worried about Mr. Mao. He is so sick. I hope he has gone to a doctor by now, which he was supposed to do. If I were the doctor, I would keep him in the hospital for tests, X rays, and rest for at least two weeks.

Tuesday, September 13

MR. MAO is better this morning. He went to the doctor
and has five different kinds of pills. He ate porridge for
breakfast, but no pickled vegetables, as he did in the
Peking airport.

At 8:15 A.M. we went to the same newspaper office
that Harrison and I had visited five years ago—*Wen Wei
Pao*. Everything looked the same: the building; the room
where we sat; the tables and chairs; the pictures of Marx,
Engels, Lenin, Stalin, and Mao—with Chairman Hua
added to the group. But all the people were different, except for Harrison and me.

As I have said before, this is where the opening shot of
the Cultural Revolution took place, when the article by
Yao Wen-yuan criticizing the play the mayor of Peking
had written was published in 1965. And until 1976, when
the Gang was smashed, this paper was a citidel of power
for the Gang.

The editors we met last time were following that line,
we were told today; they used the paper for the Gang's

propaganda, and it was dull and people didn't like to read it. Workers were criticized for working too much or too well, for paying more attention to production and less to revolutionary thought. In 1974 there was a special case of an advanced worker in a textile factory who produced 400,000 meters (437,440 yards) of unblemished material. The editors wouldn't print a story about her. After the smashing the story was published, the staff was elated, the workers in the textile factory were tremendously encouraged, production improved. Now, under the present editors, the paper is used to popularize the new party line, to spread "the right kind of propaganda." The editors we talked to last time are said to be still with the paper but doing menial work and studying their mistakes—"getting a chance to reform," they added.

We asked about the woman who was literary editor five years ago and were told that she still has the same position. We asked if we could see her, but she was out in the suburbs "organizing articles." Harrison asked what kind of articles, and the answer was, "mostly articles criticizing the Gang." During the Gang's control this paper published many pieces criticizing Premier Chou; the editors said, "We did commit bad mistakes." But recently literary articles have memorialized Chairman Mao and Chou and have "allowed one hundred flowers to bloom."

They have published stories about old actors and actresses who had not been allowed to perform since the Cultural Revolution. And a story about an overseas

Chinese man from Japan who hadn't been to China for fifty years. He left his purse containing lots of cash and bank notes in his hotel room. He was at a banquet in Nanking when the purse was returned to him. He was moved to tears. He had heard that in Shanghai there are no longer thieves. Now he saw it with his own eyes.

Also the story of the high school student who found a handbag containing thirty Swiss watches and one thousand yuan. With his parents he went to the police station and reported the find. The owner was located, a cadre from the Swiss watch factory in Chusin province. He was pleased. The boy was praised. Everyone liked to read this story. These are typical of the positive news stories published in the paper recently, we learned. (I can't help but wonder what the cadre was doing with thirty watches and so much money—more than many Chinese make in a year.)

It is confusing to me. Of the four men we talked to this morning, two were not working on the paper five years ago, and one was, though we didn't see him. I guess that means he had not been in favor with the Gang and was keeping a low profile. The fourth, Chu Hsi-chi, who had been sports editor, was in jail. In April 1968 he and some colleagues on the paper, had put up a poster criticizing Chang Chun-chiao, the boss of Shanghai and Mao's right-hand man (later a member of the Gang.) Chu Hsi-chi and forty-four others from this paper were arrested. He spent three years in jail and then was sent to a pig farm. In October 1976, when he heard over the loud-speaker that the Gang had been smashed, he threw down his shovel, jumped over the wall, and ran all the way to Shanghai. "Liberated myself," he said. He and everyone in Shanghai stayed up all night drinking and celebrating the end of the Gang, and the next day there was not a drop of *mao tai* or rice wine left in the city, he added.

Harrison asked if there is conflict between erstwhile supporters of the Gang who are still on the paper and people who were persecuted like the man above. The answer, "We must make distinctions between those people who led others to do something wrong and those who followed. Between the backbone of the Gang and those who took some part." There is also a distinction between those "backbones" who have changed their attitudes and those who haven't.

This is the same as what Ruth Coe told me, that the workers are never blamed, only the leaders.

In 1966 the circulation of this paper was 125,000. Year by year it has increased, and it has continued to grow since the smashing of the Gang. At present the circulation is 900,000. One third circulates in Shanghai, two thirds all over China. Most copies go by mail, some are sold in post offices and book and journal stores. That seems like a lot of papers to me, but H. says it is not much for the biggest city in the world with a population of more than 11 million people. The *New York Times*, for instance, has a circulation of 900,000 daily—two-thirds in New York, and one-third throughout the country. The population of New York is 7–8 million, and there are other papers. In Shanghai this is the only one. Paper is in short supply and is recycled.

But people are not dependent solely on the paper for news. Every family has a loudspeaker, as do the vegetable fields, trains, and street corners. News is broadcast constantly.

Chinese newspapers do not function as ours do. All the papers in China have the same news, sent from the central news agency, Hsinhua. Reporters don't go out and dig up stories, follow leads, or investigate politicians and government agencies. They don't have reporters in that sense. People who work on newspapers put together what they are given and do administrative work. The literary editor "organizes stories," but they are always about a good worker or a bad worker and always have a point that is sympathetic to the government line. The leading member of the editorial board of this paper, the man who "liberated" himself from the pig farm, is in charge of day-to-day political work with ideology among the staff, in liaison with upper echelons, meaning that he is in touch with and kept tabs on by higher-up cadres.

We talked about the restrictions imposed by the Gang on the cultural life. For several years Beethoven was out, an example of bad, imperialistic, capitalistic thought. Now he is back, reinstated. The Fifth Symphony has been played in Peking, though not yet here in Shanghai. The two revolutionary ballets, *The Red Detachment of Women* and *The White-Haired Girl*, are both being shown. Chiang Ching had objected to *The White-Haired Girl* because it was about one girl and her experiences, too individualistic. The opera of the same name was out or changed during her reign, but it is now being rehearsed in its original form. The *Yellow River Concerto* is not being performed, but the *Yellow River Chorus* is.

In and out, up and down, now accepted, now not. On our last visit, the incumbent editor, who is now himself out, had said to us that because Americans were exposed to so many different points of view it "must be hard for them to know what to think." Here, where the official line can change so drastically and be so heavily enforced, it must be hard for the Chinese.

Everyone we see and talk to seems elated, relieved, pleased with the turn of events. But, of course, we don't see or talk to any of the people who were on the other side.

Wherever we have gone on this visit, we have heard about the Gang of Four, the wicked things they did, the clever smashing by Chairman Hua only one month after Mao's death, the relief and joy of the people, the emerging of artists and writers, the new cultural spirit. On and on and on until really I have become tired of it. There is something so childish about the term "the smashing of the Gang." It sounds like a slapstick comedy of the 1920s or some children's game. But this afternoon at the Shanghai Music Conservatory we heard some horrifying details about the Gang's methods of stifling cultural institutions, imprisoning artists and teachers, preventing musicians from composing, performing, teaching. First we talked to members of the staff, and afterward students and one of the teachers played for us.

The Shanghai Music Conservatory was founded in 1927 and until 1949 had about one hundred students and teachers altogether. Now there are more than five hundred students and three hundred teachers. They teach piano, national instruments as well as Western, voice, orchestration—all the musical disciplines. A musical-instrument factory is attached to the conservatory. Before the Cultural Revolution primary and secondary schools were connected to the conservatory where children could be prepared for a musical-college education. These were shut down, eliminated entirely, but some day they hope to have them again. Last year they started their own training school, curiously called the May Seventh Training School, where students from eleven to seventeen years of age can study before entering the conservatory.

They told us that their students come mainly from the workers and peasants. Every primary and secondary school has a spare-time art and music school, and teachers go to those to enroll students, and to the children's palaces, which have after-school programs in many subjects as well as music. Besides musical knowledge and some skill in the arts, students are required to have good political consciousness.

Among the teachers we met with were Chou Hsiao-yen, formerly a well-known singer of classical Western music; Liu Chang-ling, famous flute player; and Lin Fuan, composer and teacher of composition.

Chou Hsiao-yen speaks English easily, spent some time in Europe in the past, and is pretty and dainty even in her drab clothes. In her sad face are signs of the treatment she received from the Gang's policies. For ten years she was not allowed to sing, not allowed to teach, not allowed to have contact with her students. However, she told us, she did manage to see them privately on Sundays and evenings, so she could encourage them and help them with their work. That is a sort of underground activity, and I can't help but wonder if some of the Gang's followers are not doing the same kind of thing today.

She was labeled "bourgeois authority," and spent the ten years doing janitor and yard work around the conservatory, and building the air raid shelters under Shanghai. She was not sent to a pig farm, but she did feed chickens.

Liu Chang-ling is especially well known as a player of folk songs on the bamboo flute (when he played for us, he used three different kinds of flutes). He was not permitted to play for years, he said, because Chiang Ching pronounced folk songs "vulgar."

Lin Fuan had a worse experience. He was kept in a room at the conservatory, was "struggled with" daily, and was not permitted to go home and see his wife for two years. Though able to see his family occasionally after that, he was still kept in his room at the conservatory for seven years more, harangued and harassed, spat upon and beaten, not allowed to see his students. By this time the conservatory was in disarray, and most students had gone out to practice revolution or work in the countryside.

The things they told us are incomprehensible, insane really. For example, Chiang Ching called herself the standard-bearer of the revolution in art and literature, proclaiming that there were only eight correct revolutionary operas and ballets and that nothing else was acceptable. Our hosts referred to her as a "pickpocket," saying she took the national heritage of music and reduced it to eight revolutionary models. They accused her of exploiting art and literature for her and the Gang's own ends. "Every field served their purpose." A few of the staff followed the Gang, but most recognized that the Gang's line was not Mao's. (This is the rub: It actually was Mao's line, but how can 900 million people be told now that Mao was the real leader of the Gang when they have been brought up to worship and revere him?)

Teachers over forty were called "decadent wood"—too old to teach. To play anything foreign meant a "worship of things foreign." The "Internationale" was the only exception. But now that they "have the eighteenth and nineteenth centuries back—we can play Bach, Mozart, and Beethoven." I asked about Russian music, and they said no Russian music is heard or taught in China now. It is mostly German, and they quoted Mao, "We must learn from the best." Imagine a music school without Tchaikovsky, Prokofiev, Rachmaninoff, Stravinsky. They know nothing of contemporary music from any country but say they are starting research into all music, including music from the Third World.

When Chiang Ching pronounced 90 percent of folk songs "vulgar," she eliminated the heart of the country's music, they said. At that point, toward the end of the Gang's supremacy, Mao criticized her, saying that "The East Is Red" (practically the Chinese national anthem) is a folk song. Here at the conservatory, folk songs as well as classical music form the basis of teaching.

The conservatory is housed in an old Jewish club that could have been a rich man's private house. Set in a spacious garden and lawn, it is in Victorian style. In a big rectangular room with heavy dark woodwork covering most of the walls and two fireplaces opposite each other on the side walls, we sat at one end in front of the windows. At the other end was a conventional grand piano.

First a student of Chou Hsiao-yen sang for us. A smiling young man, he sang folk songs in a beautiful tenor voice. Another young man banged out a piano piece that reverberated violently around the room. Since there are no rugs on the floor and no curtains to absorb the sound, it was pretty noisy. He is a capable pianist, and I would like to hear him play some of our music. (Since getting this ready for publication, Seiji Ozawa, of the Boston Symphony, has been to Peking to direct their orchestra and to teach.)

Mr. Liu played several pieces on his three different flutes, including a bamboo flute which is usually used for folk songs. He played exquisitely, with feeling and love for his music. Sitting there listening to him, looking at the other teachers, thinking of what the last ten years had been for them, it was hard to believe that these civilized, talented people had been so denied and the Chinese people so deprived of their gifts.

Tonight we were given a dinner by Lin Te-min, of the Foreign Affairs Department of the Shanghai Revolutionary Committee. Present were H. and me; Mr. Mao; our new interpreter, who really doesn't merit that term, the lady who accompanies us everywhere and who took Mr. Mao to the hospital; and our local host.

Dinner was exquisite, though not as flashy as the dinner given us by the Gang's representative five years ago. We have been told over and over that Wang spent more than twenty thousand yuan entertaining his "younger brothers" in hotels. And I guess we had an example of that in 1972.

At the table tonight the napkins were folded into the shapes of various birds and put into one of the glasses at each place. Hors d'oeuvres consisting of a big platter surrounded by several small dishes, were on a big lazy susan in the middle of the table. The big dish was composed of shrimp, meat slices, vegetable slices, and hard-boiled egg slices, in the shape of a basket of flowers. It is pretty hard to describe. It was a basket on its side; at the bottom were shredded vegetable and meat slices. The body of the basket was of meat slices in layers so that they looked like woven straw. The boiled shrimp was arranged to look like flowers coming out of the basket, and the handle was of the egg slices. The small dishes contained beans, mushrooms, cold duck slices, something fried, and tiny pieces of cold tongue.

The hors d'oeuvres were replaced by a big silver tureen of shrimp and some tender kind of nut—Mr. Mao said they were olive nuts—and potato puffs, very light and delicious. Next, duck with no trimmings except for a sort of doughy muffin, followed by a whole fish, a gorgeous platter of two kinds of dark mushrooms and Chinese cabbage, lovely and green and tender, and rice, which everyone except H. refused. Melon soup was served in the shell, on which was carved a dragon. The fruit was scooped out in balls and put into the clear soup. These melons are a cross between a dessert melon and a squash—mild and white and they taste more like a vegetable than a fruit. The dragon curved around the entire shell, and when the melon was held up to the light, it stood out green against a nearly transparent background. It was fantastic, a real work of art. How do they think of such things?

Harrison got bored and annoyed because our host wouldn't give him a definite answer about how much time Mao spent here in Shanghai, especially in the early part of the Cultural Revolution when he was not in the driver's seat. He is being played down, it seems, while the cult of Premier Chou is going strong.

There was no drinking except for two toasts, which everyone just sipped. A relief from the meals in Inner Mongolia, which I still remember with horror.

Wednesday, September 14

THIS MORNING there was a terribly heavy mist, with rain off and on. Three men, Ling Chi-hao, the director of the Shanghai Film Studio; Pai shui, director of the Shanghai Opera Theater and author of the dance drama *The Dagger Society*; and Jen Ta-lin, author and literary editor of the People's Printing House, came here to the hotel to see us. It was a long interview and at times repetitious. H. scribbled in my notebook, "If you want to excuse yourself and go to the bathroom, it's okay," meaning he thought I must be bored. But I stayed.

Mao had been in favor of a policy of realism and revolutionary romanticism, but Chiang Ching insisted on the "principle of three emphases—emphasis on positive characters, emphasis on heroism, emphasis on the main hero," they told us. Mr. Ling said that he had made some films during the Gang years—*The Brilliant Youth, Intelligence Work Across the Yangtze, Spring Sprout*, about barefoot doctors; *Second Spring*, about building warships in China designed by the Chinese. All films had to fill the requirements of the cultural department. He redid a previous film of his, *Young Generation*, which had been a favorite of Premier Chou's, but Chiang Ching did not accept it.

The Dagger Society had been one of Mao's favorite plays. It celebrated the Taiping Rebellion in 1853, the first in China against the oppressive feudal system. Mr. Pai shui told us that it was first performed in 1959, and it was played all over China until Chiang Ching banned it. In January of 1977 it was played for the first time in ten years.

Mr. Jen Ta-lin talked a long time and told several of the stories with which we have become so familiar, including "The Tortoise and the Hare," which is called "The Turtle and the Rabbit" here and is a Chinese classic. The snail-ashtray story is a true contemporary tale.

It seems that a delegation of Chinese technicians came to the United States to visit industrial establishments. At one place, as souvenirs, they were given ashtrays made in the form of a cornucopia. When they returned to China, they made their report and submitted their gifts. Chiang Ching saw the ashtrays, charged that the cornucopias were actually snails, that it was an insulting gesture meaning that the Chinese were like snails—slow, backward people. In the Politboro she urged the Chinese government to make a complaint and get the United States to apologize. Chou En-lai, still active and effective at that time, opposed this, said it was nonsense, and with some difficulty persuaded the Politboro not to do anything.

But that was not the end of the snail story. The Gang had an article published in a Shanghai magazine dealing with the incident in detail. Crazy?

It was the same old song. The Gang used films, theater, and the media to further their own ends, which is just what the present regime is doing. They suppressed good works, good writers, good artists. Mr. Jen continued working as an editor, but he didn't write anything. He spent most of his time reading the classics.

We asked if a writer or a composer can write what he wants, what he feels like, or does everything have to have a revolutionary theme? And we wanted to know if they have any interest in contemporary films and books from Europe and the United States. They talked about the Mao principle—to make the old serve the new and to make the foreign serve China. I guess those were the answers.

Driving to Fudan University after lunch we could easily understand why so many people have been wearing rubber boots (including two of the men we talked to this morning). Many streets are still flooded from the typhoon, and we had to make several detours. At one place where we were rerouted, a policeman said the water was four feet deep. Most of the old houses are built right on the street. Some have no threshold, while others have a small step between the house and the street but not high enough to keep out the water. It must be awful inside.

It seems clear that here in Shanghai "social order," as

they call it, has not been restored to what it was before the Cultural Revolution, or even in 1972. We are told that the drains are all clogged up with silt and the city is still so disorganized it hasn't been able to get them cleaned up yet. People do seem undisciplined and independent. At many street corners there are no policemen, and the traffic is unbelievable. Bicyclists come at us like a relentless ocean wave and only part for the car to go through at the very last minute.

At the university we sat in the same room we had sat in with John and Wilma Fairbank in 1972 (he is Professor of East Asian studies at Harvard) and a large group from the faculty. The only people present today who had been at that meeting were Harrison and me and Professor Ten Chi-hsing. All the others seem to have been on the wrong side and have not yet made amends, if they ever can.

This university was very much under the control of the Gang at that time, but no one referred to a "gang" in those days. It was just the Cultural Revolution. As we already knew on that visit, Mao started the Revolution to try to regain his power, and it got out of control. But no one ever said who was managing to keep it out of control; they just said that the Red Guards had taken matters into their own hands and gone too far. There was never a reference to leaders who might be promoting the turmoil. Questions we have asked everywhere are, "Why didn't people know about the Gang until it was smashed?" and "Why didn't they object, do something about what was happening if they all realize now it was so wrong?" Most people didn't dare, obviously, went along to save their skins. Only a few spoke out and were arrested or punished in some way.

It was a depressing interview. The old professor seemed very tired, cynical, and bored. Most of the talking was done by a cadre who was a teacher before the Cultural Revolution. He said he had carried out Liu Shao-chi's way and made mistakes, that he had separated theory and practice. But with the help of his comrades he has been able to resume his work. He said that when the Gang criticized Premier Chou, some people became aware that something was wrong. He himself had many suspicions about the Gang, had many questions in his mind, was not sure what was correct. He doesn't want to make the same mistakes again. He said that the Gang had prevented people from wearing black armbands when Chou died, but when I asked how could they, a young man who has studied English for two and a half years and speaks remarkably well and easily said that some students did wear black armbands and even had a simple memorial service for Chou.

This student was tall, handsome, and extremely smart, but talked the straight Marxist-Leninist line and thinks that the two-class struggle is the only problem. No matter how smart, I suppose if one is exposed to one way of thinking for twenty-five years, one is apt to believe it is the only way. He told us he studied English for one year under the Gang's control and was told he must put politics first, that to study hard was "to be white and expert."

The old professor didn't say much except when H. asked him to express his thoughts. He then said that the correct viewpoint is that all history is the story of class struggle. The Gang had held that the struggle is between Confucius and the legalist school, but the professor felt there was something wrong with that attitude. He also said that the professors and the faculty were not courageous in objecting to the Gang. Some students were, especially one girl who put up a poster praising Premier Chou. She was arrested the next day and sent down to a farm. When the Gang was smashed, people from the university went to get her, and she is studying here now, though we did not see her.

Hangchow, Thursday, September 15, before going to bed

WE GOT HERE to Hangchow last night at precisely 11:30 P.M., the exact time we were scheduled to arrive, on the train from Shanghai. The trip took three hours. Mr. Mao slept the whole way, and H. and I talked about the Gang, what we have gathered from the people we have met, how it had been for so many during the Gang's control, and the situation now.

We have been told that most people knew things were in a mess but didn't dare talk among themselves because of the general atmosphere of suspicion. It must have been similar to the McCarthy days in the 1950s in our own country, when even to have shown interest in anything connected to communism was reason enough to be hauled up before the Un-American Activities Committee and harassed and harangued just exactly the way the communists do. Although I don't know anyone who was sent to jail or killed, I know many dedicated public servants who lost their jobs, were unable to get work, and whose lives and careers were ruined for no honest reason at all.

We gather that many Chinese didn't believe Hua had the strength or ability to take the lead and restore order. They were surprised and relieved at the smashing of the Gang and now hope for peace and progress. Shanghai is very unsettled, we understand. They still can't be sure of the army, though much has been "cleaned out," which must mean that people have been purged one way or another.

The main feeling I have about the Gang and what happened between 1972 and now, is one of shock and sadness about the way Chou En-lai was treated. When he was old and ill, and right up until he died, he was criticized publicly by followers of the Gang. Posters were put up, stories against him were circulated in the media, he was reviled as a "capitalist roader," and his closest compatriot, Teng Hsiao-ping, was removed from office.

It must have been a sorrowful way to end, with a powerful clique spreading false propaganda and lies, striving to get the better of him. He, of all people, a man who went through the Revolution with Mao, from the Long March in 1936 until his death; one of the few men in the government who had some understanding of the rest of the world; a wise, clever diplomat, dedicated to the welfare of the Chinese people. It is more and more incredible to me that this happened and that the Gang was so powerful that very few dared not to follow, and fewer dared to protest.

Now Chou En-lai is being reinstated as the hero he was. In fact, in Shanghai, we heard much more about Premier Chou than about Chairman Mao. He is thought of with affection, whereas Mao is more the father figure.

Obviously in 1972, when we were here, the element that is now running the government had gotten the Cultural Revolution more or less under control. Chou was in charge and was a very active premier, and things looked better than they had since 1966, when Liu Shao-chi was gotten rid of, and then again since Lin Piao flew off in 1971 and crashed in Mongolia, as they say.

It's all the same story right up to now, and it seems to me there will always be a power struggle. Is it a question of luck who wins out, or who controls the army? Mao picked Liu Shao-chi for his successor and got rid of him when he became too powerful; named Lin Piao and got rid of him when he became too powerful and was supposedly plotting to kill Mao. He gave Chiang Ching power, or she took it because she was his wife, and he couldn't stop her. During Mao's last years she became very powerful, dictated what was to be in the art world, had a powerful group around her—the others in the Gang. But only a month after Mao's death she was arrested, along with her top followers. How did she get so much power? How did Hua have the power to throw her out? Who helps whom? Who is behind whom? Where does the army stand? What has happened to all the people who were on the Gang's side? How long will they stay submerged? Have those who were, and still are, being criticized, really changed their tune, or are they just singing the current popular hit?

We are staying in a guest house right on the West Lake. Most of the buildings are of nice dark gray brick, and the center building, built in 1951, is in traditional pagoda style. It isn't being used now except for storage. Bicycles and old furniture are stacked on this beautiful marble floor, which is spattered with paint. I wouldn't mind if a cow barn looked the way it does, but for a handsome building with marble floors and good woodwork to be such a mess is dreadful. Perhaps they will fix it up. The doors open onto a terrace and boat landing.

Our room is in a new building that looks like a three-story motel. Built of pink brick with light-green-painted balconies, it is ugly and out of place in this particular compound, where the other buildings are attractive and all of a piece. We are comfortable, but the bathroom floor has obviously never been washed, and the tub is all stained. Yet we were told that we are the first foreigners to stay here and that everything is new. Whoever is responsible for our room left a container of cleanser, which I can't see was ever used, in the bathroom, and I scrubbed a piece of the floor. The tiles came out clean and shining. So it can be done. We slept under mosquito nettings because H. feels that when they are present, it means there is a need for them. We have killed some mosquitos in the bedroom and bathroom.

Our buildings are enclosed by a high wall, and though we are only a stone's throw from the main shopping and business areas of the city, it is quiet and peaceful as if we were miles away in the country. Driving around, we noticed many villas behind similar walls with the gates closed and guarded by soldiers. One had several strands of barbed wire on top of a very high wall. I wonder who or what is behind them? The Gang is supposed to be imprisoned in the Peking area.

Hangchow and the West Lake represent what I think of as old and historic China—the land of poets and writers, artists and philosophers, of willows and lakes and jagged mountains in the background. It still has that atmosphere in spite of what has happened here.

In the early days of the revolution, Mao and Chou and other leaders spent a lot of time in Hangchow, right in this guest house compound where we are staying. Since Shanghai was Mao's headquarters off and on, especially when he was on the shelf, so to speak, Hangchow was a handy place to come to rest and plot and plan. During the last few years the city was twice closed to foreigners for six months at a time, in 1974 and 1976, because of the deterioration of "social order," as they put it. Harassment of leading members of institutions, lack of production, and disorder in the factories and in the streets were everyday occurrences. Street committees did not function, garbage piled up, streets were not cleaned, there was fighting on the railroads. Often trains to and from Shanghai did not run because of armed clashes among railroad workers. In Peking all the Chinese we talked to reiterated how good it was that we were coming to Hangchow, that after talking to people here we would be able to understand much better about the Gang.

This morning it poured rain off and on but we went sightseeing, nevertheless, to the big red Pagoda of Six Harmonies and to the Tiger Springs. At the latter place, the story goes, a monk stopped to settle, but there was no water. A fairy appeared to him and said not to be disheartened, to look for a tiger, and under it would be a source of water. The fairy was certainly right. Even if it hadn't been raining, it would have been wet. Springs, brooks, waterfalls, man-made ponds, water everywhere. Beautiful buildings, courtyards with gardens and trees, heavenly windows with birds and fish carved in the woodwork. A teahouse is built around a pond filled with enormous carp. Feeding these grotesque fish is a favorite sport of the Chinese, and the Japanese too. We were given pieces of squash to throw at them, but other places we have thrown bread. These fish get as big as three feet and are terribly fat. These particular carp are not eaten—about the only thing you could say is wasteful in this society where everything is used in some form—but are only for amusement.

Mr. Mao told us that the water is so heavy it can support a coin, and naturally we didn't believe him. With glee he asked a waiter to bring us a glass and some water. He put the glass down on the table and filled it up until the water was slightly higher than the rim, and didn't spill. Then he put a piece of money on the water, and it stayed on top. Baffling, but we had to believe him after that.

Lunch, a short rest, and a visit to a silk factory.

As usual, we had a talk with a leading cadre of the factory who turned out to be a pretty girl who looked about twenty-five years old. She is a staff member of the Revolutionary Committee. In answers to H.'s questions she spouted the party line, and he got very irritated at her. She, in turn, got irritated with him for being so persistent at trying to get some other kind of answer. But she didn't deviate, though her answers did not fit the questions.

The factory was started in 1955 but didn't really get going until 1960. Of 4,700 workers, 65 percent are women. There are three major workshops, for reeling, weaving, and dying and printing. The yearly output is 6 million meters (6,561,600 yards).

She told us that the factory had been thrown into chaos by the Gang. A reactionary, Wong Shung-hou, was smuggled into the factory, joined the party, became vice-chairman of the factory committee, and "did a lot of evil things, was a dirty dealer."

Wang Hung-wen, of the Gang, came twice to the factory, calling Wong his "younger brother." Our hostess said that he spread lies about there being contradictions between "old cadres and young cadres" and "openly twisted the party line."

She went on and on about Wong being arrogant, about his being given a position of power by the Gang and the damage he kept doing. She said he "destroyed the unity of the party; caused conflicts among the working class; destroyed the Revolution and sabotaged production." And that the Gang "fabricated charges against leading comrades." When H. asked her how she knew this, she answered, "Wong confessed when he was arrested." But that doesn't mean she knew these things were happening before his arrest, and who can tell what she thought or what all the other workers and cadres thought and believed.

She talked a great deal about "rushing promotion, rushing unprepared people to be members of the party, and cadres." She explained the "8-3-15 command of the People's Liberation Army—eight hours of work a day, three meals a day, fifteen yuan pay." The Gang didn't approve of this; it showed no political consciousness to work so hard. She told the story of the good worker who came early, stayed late, worked all the time. Followers of the Gang asked him why he stayed so late, "did he want to steal silk from the factory?" She repeated the popular statement attributed to the Gang, that to work hard was "making wedding costumes for capitalists." H. said we had heard this before, that it is not an original remark.

She had worked, at that time, in the reeling workshop. H. asked her if the Gang had tried to influence her not to work so hard. She said she was brought up in the new society, stayed in the factory, kept on working, did not "go away," as they had urged her to do. H. asked what "go away" meant, and it turned out it really meant to strike. H. said there was striking here and troops had to be called in. She said that was not true, it only appeared in the foreign press.

I got confused here and wrote in my notebook, "I am lost." She said something about putting buckets on workers' heads. It turned out that the Gang's men put baskets on workers' heads to shame them.

After even more of this pointless talk she took us on a tour of the factory. I have never been to a silk factory before, and I was fascinated. I am amazed at how many steps the silk goes through before it comes out as the finished product—as many or more steps than the wool in the blanket factory. I would think the silk would be worn out by the process. First the cocoons are washed, then there is spinning, winding, dying, drying, weaving, designs imprinted, washing again to remove the sizing, drying, pressing. We watched a plain piece of silk go through several imprinting machines. The first imprint was simply of three flowers in a cluster, repeated all over the cloth, pretty and simple. But by the time they got through adding leaves, bamboo, and birds in different colors, it wasn't half so attractive.

On our tour through the factory both H. and I noticed that our girl cadre only spoke to and smiled at one worker. With the others she was aloof and superior, clearly conscious of her improved rank.

Afterward, at a store in the city, I bought two pieces of silk for $2.50 a meter (39.37 inches). The designs are too wild for dresses, but they will make wonderful scarves to give away for Christmas.

We had dinner in the dining room of the guest house, which is a separate building on the edge of the lake. There is a wide terrace surrounded and shaded by trees, but no tables or chairs. In fact the doors are shut all the time, so we have eaten our meals indoors. Our host for dinner was the director of the Foreign Affairs Department of the Provincial Revolutionary Committee. He talked in slogans and platitudes and referred to our conversation as "this frank talk."

Friday, September 16,
on train back to Shanghai

THIS MORNING we visited a gearbox factory several miles
out of Hangchow where there had been much trouble
and great resistance to the Gang. H. had complained
about the party-line girl who took us around the silk factory yesterday, so today we had the titular head of the
factory; the real head, who is an army man; two workers;
and another party functionary.

This factory started up in 1960, was completed in 1965.
It is designed to provide all the gearboxes China needs
and some for export. There are 2,869 workers, 644 of
them women. Kindergartens, schools, and a workers'
college are attached. Seventy percent of the workers live
in new housing; there is a cinema, shops, everything one
needs. They said the standard of living is going up like
"branches on a tree."

I suppose Harrison gets something new or gets previous
statements corroborated in these discussions, but they
seem dreadfully repetitious to me. Thank heaven I have
some knitting.

Mr. Fun Ming, a party man, did most of the briefing,

and he read from a little notebook. I noticed that all the sheets he read from had been pasted onto the pages. Like our girl yesterday, he talked about the Gang "rushing admissions" to the party, "rushing promotions" to cadres. He didn't mention "rocket promotions." He told the old story about the Gang wanting their man to be secretary of the party committee even though he wasn't a member of the committee; how they ordered the incumbent secretary to go to Hangchow, but he refused. The factory stood behind him. It sounds simple now, but it really was dangerous, he said. Those people had the power and could dismiss a worker anytime.

Another episode concerning translating: I understood Mr. Mao to say that one of the workers was a bachelor, and he repeated it several times. I didn't see the significance, and it turned out he was a "bench worker." Not as funny as the confusion between *semen* and *cement*.

Chinese factories are nicely landscaped and planted around with trees, shrubs, and flowers. Yesterday at the silk factory as we walked from one workshop to the other, I was constantly impressed at the density of the trees, the cool shade they provide. How sensible it is to take advantage of natural resources to make people and buildings cooler rather than to have no trees, flat, hot roofs, paved streets and paths, no green, no shade, and air-conditioners blasting even more hot air into the streets. Plants absorb the poisonous air that factories and machines produce, so to have them is sensible as well as pleasing to the eye and other senses.

The gearbox factory is situated in a valley with hills on one side. From the room where we had our interview I could see out both directions, one side to hills and the other to bright green fields stretching on for miles. Houses have been built up the side of the hills, and it looks like a Chinese Swiss village.

In the room where we sat there were bars on the windows and locks on all the doors.

To and from the factory we drove through the most beautiful countryside—terribly green, terribly fertile, with lots of canals and ponds. It is so different from the north. Rice, cotton, jute, sugarcane—all grow enormous—and reeds and rushes are as high as the houses. The houses seem more substantial and older than those in the north, and most are decorated with pictures and designs, like barns in Pennsylvania.

There were hundreds of people on the roads, many of them pushing or pulling heavy loads. We didn't see even one cart pulled by a horse or donkey—all by people. The car honked at them unceasingly, and it made me feel awful to be sitting comfortably in a car with someone driving me while they were working so hard. We saw two water buffalo, but one was just standing on the street with a young boy on its back, and the other was grazing near the West Lake.

In the afternoon we had a ride on the lake in a small boat with an almost noiseless motor. We sat facing Mr. Mao and our local host under an awning. The lake is lovely, with mountains on the west, little islands here and there, and villas dotted around the edge. Unfortunately on the east there are smokestacks pouring out thick black smoke.

We stopped twice and walked through parks on the islands, with ponds, lakes within lakes, teahouses, and across the "nine-twist bridge," which is just what it says it is. Many Chinese were enjoying a holiday. The boat landings were busy, and many boats like ours were chugging to and fro. We were interested that we didn't go near the shore beyond our guest house, where we had noticed the guarded gates. Mr. Mao saw that I was looking at a young couple strolling on the bank, holding hands. "You didn't see that kind of thing when you were here before," he said. He was right.

We disembarked on the shore opposite where we are staying. Our car was waiting, and we drove to a huge Buddhist temple on a hill. Unfortunately the higher second hall is being renovated, but the first was wonderful and in very good condition. The four guardian statues were enormous. We met Professor Chiang Yee, of Columbia University, the author of all those wonderful "silent traveler" books—*The Silent Traveler in Boston*, . . . *in Italy*, . . . *in Scotland*, and many others. He is seventy-five years old and was climbing up and around the stone Buddhas that are carved into the caves on the hillside. His daughter is a teacher in a school near where Mr. Mao lives in Peking, but they had never met before.

In spite of his success and fame in the Western world as a writer, painter, lecturer, and teacher, Professor Chiang has had a strange and sad life. Because of a dispute with a warlord who made an under-the-counter deal with an

American oil company when he was governor of a district in China, Chiang Yee was forced to leave his country. This sounds impossible to me as an American, but he was in such bad odor with the warlord that he could find no work. He left his invalid wife and four children—two sons and two daughters—in the care of his brother and went to England, where he had one Chinese friend.

There he began by teaching Chinese but soon he was painting and illustrating and writing articles and books. After World War II he came to the United States, became a citizen, and has lived there ever since.

In 1947 he was able to get his older son to England to study printing. The son has remained, lives on the island of Jersey, and is married to a Jersey girl. The second son went to Taiwan with the Nationalist Army. The daughters and the invalid mother were cared for by relatives. Until his first trip back to his homeland in 1975 Professor Chiang had not seen his family for forty-two years.

[He died in China shortly after we returned to the United States.]

We had our supper early, and here we are on our way back to the nice hotel in Shanghai for one more night, then to Canton tomorrow afternoon.

Later, at the Ching Chin Hotel

IT IS PLEASANT to be here again. The service is so good, and it does make a difference when one is traveling to be comfortable. Sometimes I think I talk too much about toilets and bathtubs, but when you move from place to place and are on the go every minute, it helps to have things clean and in working order. We have the same room we had before going to Hangchow, and when we arrived, the floorboy brought us hot washcloths and fresh tea, just as he did every time we came in before. Tomorrow we will do some sightseeing, maybe some shopping, and we fly to Canton at 3:30 P.M.

Saturday afternoon, September 17, on the plane to Canton

FOR BREAKFAST this morning we had ice in our orange juice—the first time I've seen ice on this trip. Last time we saw one huge piece tied onto the back of a bicycle, melting as the man was hurrying home.

After breakfast we visited the Liu Yuan Gardens, a wonderful arrangement of thirty-nine buildings, court-yards, gardens, winding stairways, pagodas, little ponds, and beautiful carvings everywhere, on doors, windows, roofs, railings. Furniture in the rooms is appropriate—old and handsome.

The gardens and buildings were built in the sixteenth century by Pan Yuan-tuan, a local official, as a rest house for his father to make him happy. Unfortunately the father died before they were finished. In the opium war it was the British army camp; in 1853 it was the headquarters of the Dagger Society; and it has been destroyed several times. Before Liberation it was a bazaar. In 1956 restoration began and took six or seven years. Now it is a public park, generally thronged with people.

It was full this morning, with Chinese families enjoying a holiday. Adorable babies and children, couples acting affectionate, men playing cards in a tiny pagoda at the top of a wonderful stone stairway. They hardly looked at us when H. took their picture. Girls with curly hair, wearing brassieres, even tight skirts, and sweaters. Papers and popsicle sticks littered the beautiful gardens; there were no trash baskets to be seen or anyone making an effort to clean it up.

Driving through the narrow streets of Shanghai, we saw several women sitting in pairs at the entrances to courtyard houses. They all wore red armbands. They were Street-Committee members keeping watch on the gates to see who went in and out. This is almost the first time during this visit that street committees have been mentioned, and it is the first time we have seen any sign of them. During the Gang's period many cities, especially Shanghai, were demoralized, and street committees didn't function as they should. Now, here anyway, they are in charge again. I have always thought the street-committee plan is one of the best things about China and wish we could do something like it in our cities. If we could divide them up into smaller groups in which people would know each other, have special responsibilities, and be involved in running their own immediate communities, perhaps our cities would be more manageable.

Everyone who has been to Shanghai writes about the laundry that is hung on long poles from a window to a lamppost, or a tree, for instance, or in front of an old European mansion. Or from one house to another. Shirts are hung with the pole through the sleeves, giving them

184

shape and making them look like scarecrows.

While we waited in the lobby of the Ching Chin Hotel for Mr. Mao and our Shanghai hosts who accompanied us to the airport, we talked to one of the bellboys. He studied English in middle school, now studies by radio. He has a precise British accent, and his grammar is perfect. He is working at the hotel to improve his vocabulary. When we were leaving (our big bags were already in the car, so we only had hand luggage), he said, "Please let me help you," and carried my knitting and book bag. Lovely.

Canton, at the Feng Tang Hotel, *still September 17, 9:30 P.M.*

HOT AND TIRED as I am, I am going to write about our brief stay here and our lovely dinner, so that I won't forget anything.

On arriving at the airport we were met by another Mr. Lu, from the Reception Committee of the Foreign Office. He also speaks with a British accent. We drove to this hotel, where Harrison had stayed five years ago when he and John Lee, then Tokyo correspondent of the *New York Times*, were on their way to North Korea. At that time the hotel was huge and in two sections. Now it has two more enormous wings built around a mammoth courtyard that has tennis courts and gardens. From all the rooms on the inside you can only see the courtyard and into other people's rooms, not even a glimpse of Canton.

At the end of a trip like this our bags get unbelievably heavy from all the stuff we accumulate. Some we have bought, but most of it is books and pamphlets and papers the Chinese have given us. Our two big bags are ghastly.

I don't remember it being like this five years ago. It seemed then that everyone was helpful and obliging. I have always believed that a traveler should be able to carry his or her own bags and not bring any more than he or she can carry. I can still carry mine, but it is an ordeal. In China there don't seem to be porters as we know the term. There are always many people in the hotels sitting at desks or standing around in the halls, but usually Mr. Mao and Harrison have carried our big bags, and I carry my own stuff and the typewriter. Taxi drivers seem to be above such menial chores, and only when Mr. Mao was so ill that he could scarcely stand, did a driver offer to help. But he had to park the car, and by the time he got back, H. and I had carried everything into the airport. Maybe the past is still too close, and carrying someone's bags is too reminiscent of the feudal society, when slaves carried everything for landlords.

When we arrived at this hotel, Mr. Lu, who is small and thin, grabbed both the big bags, and going very fast, walked across the parking place (I don't know why we didn't drive right up to the door), up several steps, across a huge lobby, and into the elevator. When we got out on the seventh floor, he picked them up again, and we followed him down the longest corridor I have ever seen. Three men were sitting at a desk near the elevators, obviously hotel personnel, but not one of them moved to help him. We don't need anything that is in those bags, so they could have been checked in the lobby. But there is no facility for such a convenience.

Inside this room I feel as if I were in one of the poorer hotels in the Soviet Union. I didn't expect anything in Inner Mongolia, was grateful for any comfort. But here, where foreigners come and go all the time, where the Canton Fair is held twice a year to promote trade and income, here of all places, why can't the Chinese have a hotel that presents a better face?

Everything is grubby. The basin sticks out about an inch from the wall, obviously not installed properly, and the gap has been half filled up with regular sidewalk cement. Large gobs of it are spilled messily and stuck to the porcelain. The toilet tank (here I go again!!) doesn't fill up unless we do something to the inside each time it's flushed; that revolting drain they have on the floor is filthy, and I killed cockroaches in the bathtub.

The bedroom has two big beds, double size, covered with mosquito netting, which we will definitely use. A dressing table with a mirror, the first in China, stands across a corner with a stool in front. The surface is all scratched and stained with water marks. There are no rugs on the grimy cement floor.

The air-conditioning doesn't work, but thank heaven we have a fan, which does some good. It is hotter out than in, but it is terribly stuffy and smells of bug spray. They say they don't use DDT as they used to, but our room has been sprayed with something—even when we were in it, though I dashed out to the hall. We don't hear of malaria, but there certainly are bugs and mosquitoes. I wonder if it really has been eradicated. Certainly the whole population of Canton doesn't sleep under nets. Perhaps the Chinese are immune to the mosquitoes, which are now immune to the pesticide.

I washed out the tub, and we washed ourselves in it and went to dinner with Mr. Lu. Mr. Mao was already at the restaurant waiting with our host. He looked relaxed and smiling, said he didn't have to be the interpreter because of Mr. Lu, that this was not a working dinner, but purely for pleasure.

Our host was Mr. Yuan. That name always amuses me, as if an American were called Mr. Dollar. He is the foreign-affairs representative of the Kwantung Provincial party, or Revolutionary Committee. He is a big, friendly man and was a lovely host.

The restaurant was the Pan Hsi ("beside the sea") restaurant. It is a huge complex of courtyards, with tables set under the shading trees. It was filled with Cantonese, whole families with many babies and small children, enjoying a Saturday night supper out. Most of the men were in their undershirts, the kind that look like the bathing-suit tops my father used to wear. The Cantonese love to eat, and they think a lot about and spend a great deal of time eating. This restaurant can handle ten thousand diners, they told us, and has a staff of four hundred. I should think they'd need more.

As in all Chinese restaurants, we did not eat with "the

people." Up some stairs are three airy, open rooms—the dining room in the middle and reception or tearooms on each side. We had tea for a while, then moved to the dinner table. It was like being in a tree house, and because everything was open and we could see and hear all the jollity below, we didn't feel quite as cut off as if we had been in a private dining room with the door shut.

Dinner was still another exquisite experience. Unlike any other Chinese meal we have had, a girl served us from the platter or dish in the middle of the table. With a pretty silver ladle she gave us each a helping; after that, if we wished, we could help ourselves. But she usually anticipated our desires and served us a second time. The menu consisted of hors d'oeuvres of black eggs, some quartered, some sliced; and pieces of duck, sausage, and ham very black and crisp—all on a bed of shredded carrots. A succession of unimaginable delicacies followed—broccoli and mushrooms with tiny fish balls, steamed shrimp dumpling, chicken smoked with tea leaves, squash soup with tiny shrimp, crispy egg roll, two crispy things on a bed of shredded potato, rice mixed up with bits of ham and scrambled egg slices. We were served a cup of tea at this point, the first time we have ever had tea with a meal in China. Dessert was waterchestnut gelatinous cake, moon cake, and fresh pineapple and apples. The only flaw in this heavenly, restful evening was the chicken's head on the platter with the smoked chicken. It, too, had been smoked and was dark brown and looked as if it were made of wood.

Mr. Mao was right. It was a nice farewell dinner, no

talk of the Gang, Lin Piao, Lui Shao-chi, Chiang Ching, Taiwan, or any other problem. Now to bed in this revolting room. I anticipate a sleepless night, boiling and suffocating under the netting.

Sunday, September 18,
on the train to Hong Kong

LAST NIGHT was as expected, but breakfast was a pleasant surprise. Mr. Lu told us that visitors had been complaining that it took over an hour to get breakfast, and he advised us to get up very early, because our train left at 8:30 A.M. But we were later than usual getting up, probably because of the restless night, and didn't get to the dining room until 7:45. It was chock full of big, fat European women in low-cut and sleeveless dresses or tight pants over large, protruding derrieres and equally large men in shorts. Amazing to see after the modesty and uniformity of the Chinese dress. They must have been there for the hour it takes to get breakfast, because all kinds of eggs, omelets, toast, and coffee were coming from the kitchen, and we had our breakfast in about fifteen minutes.

Mr. Mao and Mr. Lu put us and our luggage on the train. It was sad to say good-bye to Mr. Mao, or Ta Mao, as he suggested we call him but I never could. It didn't seem natural to me. "Big Mao," it means, because though he is thin as a rail, he is tall for a Chinese (nearly 6 feet). I told him we were leaving a big piece of our hearts with him, and it's true. We became so fond of him. He was always pleasant, even when he was so sick he could hardly stand. Always thoughtful, always receptive to our wishes, our ideas, our humor; understanding and appreciative. We were with him every day for over four weeks, and you can't help but get to know quite a lot about a person living under those close conditions, even though he is ruled by an iron discipline and can't show his feelings or talk freely as we can.

I don't know how to define or describe the feelings that China and the Chinese we have come to know even so slightly evoke in me. Affection, love, sadness, pity; a maternal feeling because there is so much that is childlike in their system, customs, and behavior.

But I also feel anger against their system of government, in spite of the tremendous achievements since 1949. I resent the restrictions imposed on everyone; the constant talk about "the people," how they think, feel, and react. It is obvious that they think, feel, and especially *act* the way they are told to, and have to for their survival.

I have written before about leaving friends in the Soviet Union, and I feel the same way about leaving China. When, if ever, will we see our Chinese friends again? When, if ever, will we hear from them? (Madame Soong is the only one who writes to us.) Perhaps it is unwise for a Chinese to write to a foreigner. We write to them, send books and music; if it is safe now, will it be next year? Policy can change—what is okay today may not be tomorrow. We are welcome now, will we be in a year or so? And the friends we have made—will they be in favor or out? In this kind of government *out* means "really out." It isn't like being an Adlai Stevenson or a Hubert Humphrey, defeated for one position but able to hold another one of extreme importance. It means being relieved of all responsibility, all participation, under arrest or down to the pig farm.

Tears came to my eyes as we said good-bye here at our seats on the train. I never dare hug or kiss a Chinese, because they are so undemonstrative and reserved in public, but I certainly felt like hugging Mr. Mao. As we pulled out, we waved to him and Mr. Lu standing on the platform until we couldn't see them anymore.

Sunday night, still September 18, at the Mandarin Hotel, Hong Kong

THE TRAIN TRIP to the border, Shum Chun, was pleasant, and the countryside looked as green and calm as I remembered it. Trees have grown up on the hills, part of the Chinese reforestation efforts, and there seemed to be more people sitting on their haunches under trees. Our cowboys sit like that, but somehow they look more vigorous. When Orientals sit that way, it seems to denote endless fatigue and boredom and the same life going on day and after day after day.

The Customs people were terribly polite. As before, they didn't open anything, simply asked us what we had in our bags and took our word for it. Our bags were carried over the famous bridge that so many foreigners have now walked across, and were picked up by a British man, who led us to the waiting train.

The difference in atmosphere in that short distance, from one side of the border to the other, is staggering. The lack of "social order," of discipline, the feeling that people are individuals and not just an anonymous part of a huge whole, the color, the feeling of freedom—one senses it immediately. The train was grubby but not dirty. No tables for tea, but women and children selling ice-cold Coca-Cola. The first sip was almost divine. Signs and posters advertised cigarettes and liquor, not government propaganda. It was exciting to see a rather cheap picture of a pretty blond girl looking from a poster telling us to be sure to buy a certain kind of perfume to insure happiness and success. Or another about a trip you could take without permission. But the best is always newspapers, unregulated, free-enterprise newspapers, not carbon copies of a totalitarian news agency.

September 20, on Plane to Tokyo

WE HAVE HAD two heavenly days at one of my favorite
hotels in the world. I wrote the manager that staying at
the Mandarin is one experience that is never a disap-
pointment. Everything about it is just what a hotel
should be. The service is excellent, the food delicious.
There are many different kinds of restaurants, many
shops with tempting and beautiful things to buy or just
look at and long for, two book stores with books one
wants to read in many languages. Linen sheets are fresh
every day; everyone is friendly and polite. The newsstand
in the lobby stocks magazines, paperback books, and
newspapers from everywhere. It is a perfect place to end
a trip, to rest and relax and realize that there is another
world outside China. When I am in China, I often forget.

And now here we are, on the way home. Lying on that
hard bed in Silinhot, I thought this day would never
come. We drove to the airport with an American
businessman who had just been in Peking, staying at the
Peking Hotel. He said the food was awful and the service
very poor. In the dining room they brought him

195

something he had not ordered and were unobliging and loathe to change it. He complained about beer being left out on the serving table so that even if it started out cold, by the time he got his, it was hot. I am so used to this now it doesn't seem odd to me, though I agree, beer is much better cold than hot, and if it is possible to chill it, I would think it could be served that way.

We have never run into anything like what this man told us. Everyone has always been polite and helpful to us. But it is true that in the two cities where foreigners come so often, Peking and Canton, and especially Canton, where the fair is so important for trade and exchange, the Chinese could spruce up their hotels and make visitors more comfortable. I wonder why they don't. They should "learn from" the Shanghai Hotel.

We get to Tokyo in three hours, wait there for four more, then fly direct to New York. After being home for a while I wonder what of this trip will remain with me the clearest. Probably the whole Mongolian scene, the landscape, the Chinese influence there, the changing life of the people. But with individuals there is no question. It will be Chou Hsiao-Yen, the music teacher at the Shanghai Music Conservatory who was not allowed to sing or teach for nearly ten years. I will never forget her.

Later, in New York City

NOTHING STANDS still in China. Since our return many of the portents have become reality. There has been a rise in wages; tourists and visitors have increased by leaps and bounds. (In fact, a group just back said that the Chinese had run out of interpreters and that they had had a university professor with them for two weeks. They felt they had gained by the lack.) Almost every week I hear of someone going to China, most in groups but a few traveling alone with a guide, the way we did. Relations between our two countries seem to be progressing. There is talk of exchanging scientific know-how. Both sides appear to be more reasonable about solving the Taiwan situation. Dr. Hatem has been in New York, the first time in thirty-nine years. Girls and women are permitted, even urged, to wear colors and pretty blouses. Some are wearing skirts. There is rumor that Chinese couples may soon be indulging in "body contact" dancing.

In 1972 we were told that under the present Chinese system there is no room for neurosis, that no one was mentally ill. Now they show foreign medical groups their mental hospitals. It is safe to assume that every large city has a mental hospital, and we have been told that schizophrenia is their biggest mental problem.

In 1972 we asked and asked about a man who was a friend of a friend in the United States. This man was, and is, prominent, and everyone must have known where he was, but we never got any direct answer. It was always, "he is out of the city," "out of the province," "he is working in the countryside," or even "we don't know where he is." Recently an American wanted to see the brother of a Chinese friend who lives in the United States. There was hemming and hawing, stalling and making excuses. Eventually she became angry and said, "You must show more consideration for overseas Chinese. They want to hear about their relatives. Why do you object to my seeing this man?" And finally, on the last day of her visit, too late for her to be able to visit him in his home, he was brought to her hotel. He was very well dressed compared with the average Chinese, and when she reported this to his brother back home, the brother said, "He always did spend too much on his clothes." But that isn't really possible now in China. Perhaps he was dressed up especially to take back a good impression.

He talked openly about how he and his family had hated what was going on during the Cultural Revolution. He said that his daughter had been taken out of school and sent down to the countryside "to make revolution," whatever that means. He said that now, with the Gang smashed, everything is much better and she is back in school continuing her education.

People speak frankly of their feelings against communes, against such regimentation, but they don't speak this way if another Chinese is within earshot.

Chou Hsiao-yen, of the Shanghai Music Conservatory, went with other Chinese musicians to Stuttgart to actually hear and learn about German music. Later she came to New York with the Chinese Performing Arts Company as a deputy leader, and the Mongol dancer Modegema danced her famous bowl dance. If anyone, either on that airplane to Huhehot or on that hot September day in Shanghai, had said that the next time we saw these two ladies, it would be at the Metropolitan

Opera House in New York City, I would have thought they were crazy, insane. Yet there they were, at the end of the performance, up on the stage smiling and waving and clapping.

We talked with them afterward, and when Harrison and I had to leave, I said to Chou Hsiao-yen, "I never dare kiss a Chinese," whereupon she embraced us both.

Little by little, perhaps, our relationships with these remarkable people will become more normal. Little by little maybe we will be able to communicate back and forth and share ideas and knowledge. Changes since 1972 have been profound; you could say there has been a new kind of a "Great Leap Forward." I hope it will continue.

TRAVEL TIPS

I HAVE READ through my travel tips from *China Diary* and believe they are as appropos today as they were at that time. The only thing I would add is that it is acceptable now to take along a few presents to give away. Formerly that custom was frowned on, but paperback books, cigarettes, and other simple gifts are all right.

Any woman who has traveled a lot has her own special ideas about what is necessary to pack. While, obviously, the point in travel is to see and learn as much as possible, there is no reason not to be as comfortable as one can be without overburdening oneself. More Americans will be going to China from now on, and I thought some of my ideas might be a help.

I never go away for a weekend without a hot water bottle, nailbrush, and a baby pillow. They can easily be squashed into any bag. And I never go on a real trip in my own or any other country without three folding plastic hangers and a stretchy line to hang things on in the bathroom. In the Soviet Union a rubber stopper for tubs and basins is necessary, but not in China. Though some of the bathrooms weren't very attractive, nothing was missing. But take your own washcloth. These are not supplied. Chinese toilet paper is crepey compared with ours, but it is okay. However, as in all countries, you may be caught in a place where there isn't any. Carry a small package of tissues in your pocket or bag.

For the woman who likes pants, clothes are no problem in China. Two daytime pairs of pants, three interchangeable tops, and one outfit for evening are all you will ever need, no matter how long you stay. If you will be seeing people in the embassies, dining out a lot with foreigners, hobnobbing with other visitors, or if you are unhappy wearing the same thing every day and night, take more, or take a dress for a change, but you don't need to. Remember that all the Chinese men and women, wear the same thing day after day, and at night. And if you do much traveling around the country, you will be thankful if you don't take too much. It is best to be able to carry your own bag. If it is heavy, you may find a Chinese girl, much smaller than you, struggling with it, and that can be embarrassing. If you are unhappy in slacks, I suggest two medium-length skirts for day and a long one for evening with suitable tops. The first time I went to Asia, I took a cotton suit with elbow-length sleeves, sleeveless tops, and a short, narrow skirt. I learned my lesson quickly, had two skirts made in Delhi, one medium and one long, and hardly wore anything else the rest of the trip. Asian women dress to be comfortable and protected in their climate, so when it's hot, things are long to keep out heat and dust. In winter and cold, padded and lined layers are added.

Personally, I don't think it's appropriate to wear bare, short, or tight and revealing clothes when native women dress modestly. I don't think we should copy other women, we should be ourselves. But it's more attractive not to be any more conspicuous than we are anyway. We should remember that until recently this generation of Chinese hasn't seen many Americans, and we should give a good impression of our country. Clinging wools and knits that we wear at home are not appropriate, neither are they comfortable for travel. Something slightly loose is always better. By avoiding the extreme, a Western woman can look smart and neat even when simply dressed.

A raincoat and sweater are considered "musts" for travel in any country, at any time of year, yet in the six weeks we were in China in 1972, I wore neither and this year I only needed a sweater in Mongolia. I wore what I call sneakers (Harrison calls them tennis shoes, but any light, fabric shoes with rubber soles would be the same) nearly every day, with socks, and Harrison was sorry he hadn't brought his. They are ideal for tramping around the communes and factories. Daytime sandals, for less-strenuous sightseeing, a dressier pair for evening, and the shoes I traveled in were all I took. If I were to go in winter, I would take boots. Incidently, be careful of synthetics and man-made materials. With the exception of some forms of cotton/dacron or cotton/polyester, they make you sweaty and sticky in the heat and don't keep you warm when it's cold, though some coats do keep out the wind. Once I took to Outer Mongolia one of those quilted, puffy raincoats that are advertised as ideal traveling coats for all weather. Every time I put it on, it was like getting into a cold bed—I had to warm up the coat; it didn't do it for me. Real wool and cotton are best.

There is no risk of theft in hotels, so you can take jewelry if you want to. I didn't take any except my wedding ring, a simple wristwatch, and several identical pairs of inexpensive pearl earrings (because I lose one so often), which I wore at night when I felt like it. The clothes I took didn't require any jewelry, and as Chinese women don't wear any at all, I didn't bother. Some older Chinese women wear gold hoops in their pierced ears, but you never see anything on younger ones. However, very pretty rings and things are now made in China, and you can buy them in the friendship shops, which are especially for foreigners. We also had a small traveling clock with an alarm, cameras, a shortwave radio, and a typewriter, all of which we could leave anywhere—in airports, stations, or on top of our bags outside a hotel without worrying that someone would take anything.

For any length trip I take three sets of underclothes and two nightgowns, and I prefer color or prints because they don't get grubby and gray looking. A wrapper that is presentable in a hotel room no matter who happens to come in is a necessity, and slippers. In China, slippers are supplied on trains and in hotels, but it's nice to have your own.

I washed my clothes at night, and they were dry in the morning. Hotel laundries are fast and good for men's clothes but are a bit hard on things. I took some detergent in tiny bags but found I could buy excellent washing powder in the hotel shop. I also took some individual shoeshine packets, and they came in very handy, especially for Harrison's shoes. Dry cleaning is available in all cities and takes about five days to a week—in hotels, generally twenty-four hours.

I washed my own hair because I prefer to, and either slept with it rolled up or took some time in the morning to fix it. Most of the time I wore it twisted up under a scarf by day and merely pulled back in a barrette at night, so it didn't need much "doing." But in the hotels in Peking there are adequate beauty shops for visitors.

The only things I would do differently if I had my trip to take over again would be to read more, to study as much about China as I could and to take only the bare essentials, with me, as I have listed.

A Few Do's and Don'ts for Visiting China

Do as much homework as possible before you go. Read everything you can, past and present.

Do take a guidebook. Nagel's is the best at present. It gives some past history and lists old sights and buildings that might be overlooked.

Do always ask if it is all right to take pictures, especially in the vicinity of airports, stations, bridges.

Do take whatever you want to read, because there are no newsstands in China and no foreign magazines or novels.

Do take gin, whiskey, or whatever you prefer if you can't live without them, but they're heavy and a nuisance. It's best get used to Chinese drinks.

Don't forget that you are a traveling exhibit of American culture. Most Chinese have not seen many Americans. You may form their ideas of us and our country.

Don't expect to be an independent tourist. Realize that while you may ask for anything, the Chinese will decide where you go and what you see.

Don't make a fuss if you can't see what you want. You'll only meet a blank wall. Remember, you can't change the system.

Don't expect to be able to wander around freely in any communist country. Sometimes you can, more often not.

Don't try to do too much. Rest when you can.

Don't eat too much until you are accustomed to the changes of food, drink, and weather.

Don't drink too much *mao tai*. It is stronger than you think, well over 130 proof.

Don't bother to take cigarettes. The Chinese have many

brands, don't seem to be fearful of the dangers as we are, and many smoke like chimneys.

Don't be afraid to have your hair done in the beauty salons in the hotels.

List for Women—Summer

Two pairs of washable pants for day, or two skirts
> Cotton/dacron is best; polyester gets heavy and hot, but it does keep its shape.

Three tops to wear with the above—washable
> I prefer tops that are worn outside. They are cooler and usually more becoming.

Pants or long skirt for evening

One or two tops
> Take Banlon or something synthetic, because it's bearable at night, washes and dries easily, and doesn't wrinkle.

Sweater

Raincoat

Wrapper

Slippers—terry cloth slippers are ideal for hot places.

Underclothes—your own preference

Nightgown—your own preference

Scarves for head and hair to cover and keep out wind and dust
> Two are plenty because you can buy pretty silk ones.

Umbrella

Optional because you can buy them, or parasols for sun, or big straw hats for about eighty cents.

Shoes

Sneakers or simple, comfortable fabric shoes with rubber soles for walking in communes and factories.

Sandals for daytime when not so strenuous
Sandals or shoes for evening

Small bag in case you go on an overnight trip and don't have to take everything

List for Women—Winter

Just about the same as above, only heavier, warmer clothes

Wool pants suit and extra pants that can be worn with the suit jacket

Or suit and extra skirt that can be worn with the suit jacket

Several tops

Two sweaters

Evening outfit, slacks, or skirt and appropriate tops

Woolen stole to go with above, and for use in day

Heavy weatherproof or storm coat

Woolen hat or cap, gloves, scarves

Boots, warm and waterproof

Shoes for sightseeing

Shoes for evening

Wool wrapper

The thin knitted kind, lined with silk, are ideal for traveling. They are expensive, but last for years and take up very little room.
Slippers

List for Men—Summer

Two pairs of washable pants
One lightweight suit—can be drip-dry
Shirts and sport shirts (remember, the laundry comes back the same day)
Sneakers or fabric rubber-soled shoes
Two pairs of other shoes
Sandals—if you like them
Raincoat
Sweater
Underclothes, etc.—personal
Bathrobe and slippers—optional

List for Men—Winter

Two suits
Two sweaters
Warm weatherproof coat
Hat or cap, scarves, gloves
Bathrobe and slippers
Underclothes, etc.—personal

Things You Can Buy in China

Toothbrushes and toothpaste
Shampoo
Shaving cream, etc.
Soap
Detergent
Socks
Sweaters
Sandals
Straw hats
Plastic raincoats
Umbrellas
Silk scarves
In the friendship stores for foreigners you can buy cosmetics, but they are probably not what you would prefer. However, they do sell the following:
Cold cream
Lipstick
Face powder
Talcum powder
We even saw some wigs for about $10

Things You Should be Sure to Take

Aspirin
Kleenex
Absorbent cotton if you use it to remove cream or apply lotion

Creme rinse for hair
Tampax
Any special medicine
Any special cosmetics
Washcloth
Pantyhose or nylon stockings
Prescription for glasses, or extra pair
Instant coffee or Sanka—hot, boiled water is always available, so is tea, but their coffee doesn't appeal to many Americans.
Film—you can buy only slow black and white, no color.

Not necessary, but if you can, take a shortwave radio. When the country, the people, the language—everything—is strange to you, there is nothing so comforting as *The Voice of America* or the nursery jingle that starts the BBC daily broadcasts.

INDEX

American interest in China has skyrocketed with "normalization" of Chinese-American relations, the establishment, after thirty years, of normal diplomatic, cultural and trade relations.

Charlotte Y. Salisbury has made five trips in the past dozen years to China and its borderlands. With her husband, Harrison E. Salisbury of *The New York Times*, she was one of the first to enter the People's Republic of China after President Nixon's 1972 trip.

Now she has again traveled extensively in China in the months before the spectacular explosion of pro-American sentiment and assertions of sympathy for democracy which accompanied "normalization" and the dramatic rise of China's new leader, Teng Hsiao-ping.

She records her impressions of this China in ferment in *China Diary: After Mao* with the same sensitive observer's eye that marked her earlier *China Diary*, written during her 1972 trip, and her *Asian Diary* and *Russian Diary*.

Her travels take her to Inner Mongolia, where she is able to contrast and compare Mongols living in China with life in Outer Mongolia across the border where she